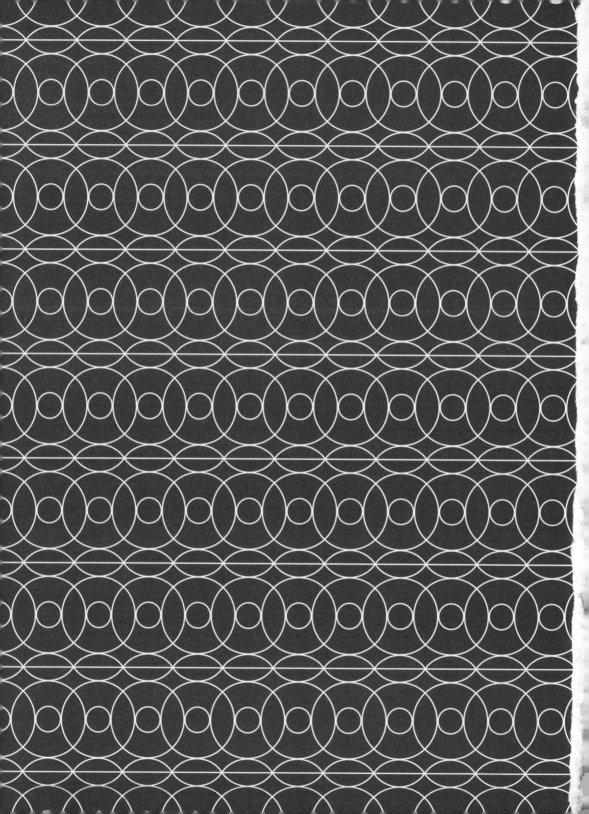

Best **Lunch Box** Ever

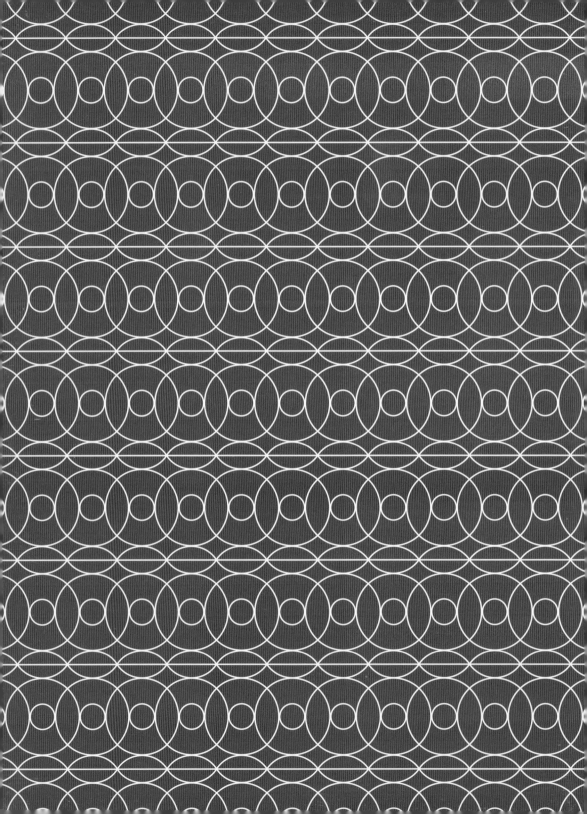

BEST LUNCH BOX EVER

IDEAS AND RECIPES
for School Lunches
KIDS WILL LOVE

KATIE SULLIVAN MORFORD

PHOTOS BY **JENNIFER MARTINÉ**

CHRONICLE BOOKS
SAN FRANCISCO

For my girls

Text copyright © 2013 by Katie Sullivan Morford.
Photographs copyright © Chronicle Books LLC.

Library of Congress Cataloging-in-Publication Data available.

ISBN 978-1-4521-0829-2

Manufactured in China

FSC
www.fsc.org

MIX
Paper from
responsible sources
FSC® C016973

Designed by Eight Hour Day
Photographs by Jennifer Martiné
Food styling Karen Shinto
Prop styling by Leigh Noe

10 9 8 7 6 5 4 3 2 1

Chronicle Books LLC
680 Second Street
San Francisco, California 94107
www.chroniclebooks.com

Contents

Introduction

Why a Lunch-Box Book?

My friend Pam, a mother of two, can practically turn out a dozen golden popovers with her eyes shut. Claire, also a mom, tackles even the most sophisticated recipes with the ease of a professional. And Suzanne churns out family dinners each night in such an orderly fashion, she could teach Martha Stewart a thing or two. But ask any of these übercapable moms—or dads, grandparents, or other caregivers, for that matter—how they feel about packing school lunches every day and you are likely to hear a groan, a sigh, or, quite possibly, a growl.

WHAT GIVES?

First off, packing lunch is a relatively thankless task; we aren't even around when the kids crack those containers open. Plus, filling a lunch box is booby-trapped with challenges: keeping some foods hot and others cold, preventing sandwiches from going mushy and fruit from bruising, figuring out what kids will like (and eat!), and doing it all in the few extra minutes of the day you really don't have. And that's not even taking into account the folks who have to work around a kid's food allergy or a ten-year-old who's suddenly gone vegan. Phew! It's a lot to cover. With three daughters of my own, I've packed roughly 4,000 lunches and counting. It's not easy, but I've learned a thing or two along the way.

This book brings together my expertise as a registered dietitian, food writer, and cooking teacher with my hands-on experience as a parent. My aim is to arm you with easy recipes and practical advice for lunches your kids will actually eat instead of toss in the trash.

All of the recipes are based on how we do things around our house. Good ingredients and simple preparation are the foundations of my cooking, with an eye to nourishing kids, not just filling them up. I rely largely on seasonal organic produce; sustainably raised eggs, dairy, fish, poultry, and meat; and whole grains. Convenience foods such as jarred applesauce and prepared soups fill in as needed. While I'm not churning butter from my own grass-fed dairy cows, I'm also not buying fried snack foods in bulk. It's a balancing act.

This book is a toolbox full of fresh ideas to help you break from the lunch-box rut that plagues the best of us. Most of the recipes are quite flexible, intended for tinkering to suit your family's preferences and whatever happens to be in your pantry. Capers too fancy? Use chopped relish. Tofu too "health foodie"? Substitute chicken. Chocolate chips not "health foodie" enough? Leave 'em out. Your child, your cooking, your lunches.

My hope is that this book is approachable. When it's not, please tailor the recipes to suit you. Whether your offspring is four or fourteen, the idea is that the *Best Lunch Box Ever* should inspire you so that making lunches can be a little more joyful and less of a chore.

CHAPTER 1

Brown Bag Basics

WEEKDAY MORNINGS CAN BE DOWNRIGHT NUTTY. On some days, the fact that you manage to pull a lunch together at all feels like a minor miracle, never mind if it has much in the way of nutritional value. And what does a nourishing lunch really look like anyway?

This chapter is intended to help you understand just that. Through practical nutrition advice and food safety tips, packing healthful lunches can become second nature, even in the chaotic rush of school-day mornings. I've included a comparison of traditional school lunches with new and improved versions to illustrate how little changes in ingredients can make a big difference in nutrients (see Give Lunch a Makeover, page 17). Perhaps this will encourage you to make a few tweaks in your kitchen that result in more wholesome packed lunches.

Know Good Nutrition

There's no getting around the fact that pulling together a healthful school lunch is a worthy pursuit. What children eat during the school day puts a significant dent toward meeting their dietary needs, so you gotta make it count. While a bag of cheese puffs, can of soda, and salami on white might fill them up, it's not truly nourishing them. You can deliver those same calories with a lot more nutrition, which today's kids definitely need. Consider this: According to the USDA, the diets of more than 80 percent of kids between the ages of two and nine need substantial improvement. Yikes!

Here's what a nutritious, well-thought-out school lunch can do for kids:

- Fuel their brains so they can focus in class.
- Support growth and development.
- Promote healthful eating habits.
- Energize them to participate to their fullest in everything from physics to phys ed.
- Provide fiber, vitamins, minerals, and other key nutrients.
- Help them maintain an appropriate weight.
- Offset moodiness.
- Let them know how much you care, especially if you include a loving note or other thoughtful gesture.

So what really needs to be packed in that lunch box to ensure it's well balanced?

Start by emphasizing fresh, seasonal, whole food that has spent more time on a farm than in a manufacturing plant. Cobbling together a nutritious lunch gets a lot easier if you rely on real food from the get-go. It needn't be complicated or scientific. Here's the lowdown on the building blocks of a healthful midday meal.

WHOLE-GRAIN FOODS

Whether it's the whole-wheat bread on a sandwich or the brown rice in a stir-fry, whole grains are the core of a solid school lunch. These complex carbs provide the quickest form of energy and are the number-one fuel for those hardworking brains. Whole grains take longer to digest than processed ones, supplying your child with a steady source of energy.

Using whole grains is key since they haven't been stripped of the bran and germ (and the nutrients that go along with them). Don't be duped by deceptive marketing. Many foods made from grains, breads in particular, get paraded around as if they are more healthful than they are. Read the label and look for the word *whole* as in *whole wheat* instead of just *wheat*.

Grocery and specialty stores now stock an array of grains from which to choose: barley, farro, quinoa, oats, bulgur wheat, brown rice, spelt, amaranth, teff, buckwheat, and millet. You can also buy a huge variety of whole-grain pastas and breads. And get this: Popcorn is a whole grain, too. How cool is that?

PROTEIN FOODS

It's essential to balance grains with protein-rich foods, which provide important nutrients and help to keep blood sugar steady so your child doesn't bottom out in class. Protein also stimulates brain activity, promoting the alertness necessary for a successful school day.

The likes of meat and chicken usually come to mind when we think of protein, but plant-based foods shouldn't be overlooked. Choosing, say, black beans over ground beef for example, costs less, and they're lower in unhealthful fats. Plus, they're gentler to the environment since growing beans produces less greenhouse gases than raising and processing meat.

Protein-rich lunch box–friendly foods include beans, lentils, chickpeas, split peas, peanuts, nuts, nut butters, seeds, seed butters, tofu, tempeh, soybeans (edamame), soy nuts, milk, yogurt, cheese, cottage cheese, eggs, chicken, turkey, pork, beef, lamb, sardines, shrimp, salmon, and tuna.

HEALTHFUL FATS

Fats get a bad rap despite the fact that they are necessary for health and have a place in a balanced diet. Fats not only carry essential vitamins, they can actually increase the absorption of nutrients from other foods. Oh, and those healthy omega-3s you're always hearing about? Those are fats found in foods such as walnuts, canola oil, flaxseeds, and salmon.

On a more practical front, fats may help us feel satiated since they take their sweet ol' time to digest. Add a smear of pumpkin seed butter to your child's jam sandwich, and it will likely fill him up a whole lot longer.

While it's important not to turn your skinny nose up at fats, be smart about the types you choose and how much of them you serve to your child. Certain fats are better for you than others, which I've spelled out below. Keep in mind that all fats are high in calories, so love your almond butter, but don't go swimming in it.

Better fats. Avocados, nuts and nut butters, seeds and seed butters, olives, sardines, and salmon are all rich in healthful fats, including (in a few cases) the coveted omega-3s.

Best to minimize. Fatty processed meats such as salami, hot dogs, bacon, and sausage; heavily marbled beef and other rich meats; and palm oil, palm kernel oil, and fully hydrogenated oils are all sources of saturated fat and should be kept in check. The same goes for full-fat dairy products, including heavy cream, butter, whole milk, and full-fat cheeses.

Skip altogether. Many margarines, baked goods, and snack foods are made with partially hydrogenated vegetable oils, ingredients known as trans fats. These oils are considered particularly unhealthful because they both raise your "bad" cholesterol and lower your "good" cholesterol. Keep them out of your shopping cart entirely.

DID YOU KNOW?

Greek-style yogurt has about double the protein of regular yogurt.

FRUITS AND VEGETABLES

It's tricky to meet the USDA's recommendation that half of our plates be filled with fruits and vegetables. If we've got any hope of reaching that goal, some of that produce has got to show up at lunch. Getting a couple of fruits and veggies in during the school day isn't as challenging as you might think. If you include, say, a generous thermos of vegetable soup and a lovely ripe peach in a school lunch, you've knocked out 1½ cups of produce right there. Not bad.

Also, aim for variety rather than choosing the same foods over and over again. Be sure to tap into every hue of the fruit-and-vegetable rainbow. Offering your child a colorful mix of produce means they'll take in a broad range of nutrients. For example, orange vegetables tend to be high in beta-carotene, dark leafy greens are typically rich in folic acid, and purple foods are often packed with anthocyanins, a powerful antioxidant.

ORGANIC OPTIONS

Fruits and vegetables are a must, but which ones? Ideally, buy produce grown without pesticides, which is better for the environment, better for farming communities, and better for your kids.

If routinely buying organic isn't accessible, either economically or practically, have a look at the Dirty Dozen and the Clean 15, two useful lists developed by the folks at the Environmental Working Group that can help you decide where to put your organic food dollars.

DIRTY DOZEN

It's best to opt for organic when buying these fruits and veggies since they tend to have the highest levels of pesticide residues:

apples	peaches	grapes (imported)	blueberries (domestic)
celery	spinach	bell peppers	lettuce
strawberries	nectarines (imported)	potatoes	kale/collard greens

CLEAN 15

These fruits and vegetables are your best bets when buying conventionally grown produce since they tend to have the lowest levels of pesticide residues:

onions	asparagus	cantaloupes (domestic)	sweet potatoes
sweet corn	peas	kiwis	grapefruits
pineapples	mangoes	cabbages	mushrooms
avocados	eggplants	watermelons	

CALCIUM-RICH FOODS

Many kids today drink more soda than milk, which is just one of the reasons they may not be getting enough calcium. Children need three to four servings of milk or other calcium-rich food or drink a day. Send your child to school with yogurt and a sandwich with a slice of cheese, and you've already met about half of their daily needs.

Here are a handful of high-calcium sources, which offer about one-quarter to one-third of the daily requirements, depending on a child's age. (Be aware that calcium levels can vary by manufacturer.)

1 cup nonfat milk

1 cup calcium-fortified soy milk

1½ ounces Cheddar, mozzarella, or Muenster cheese

½ cup part-skim ricotta cheese

⅔ cup plain nonfat yogurt

1 cup chopped cooked spinach

1 cup calcium-fortified orange juice

⅓ cup instant nonfat dry milk powder

Other good calcium sources include dried beans, chickpeas, almonds, calcium-fortified breakfast cereals, broccoli, kale, turnip greens, okra, bok choy, and canned sardines. You can boost calcium further by adding a spoonful or two of nonfat dry milk powder to soups, baked goods, puddings, and casseroles.

DRINKS

Colorful juice boxes, shiny drink pouches, and flavored milks are awfully tempting for kids. Slipping one into the lunch box on occasion is a fine way to keep things interesting, but these beverages should be seen for what they are: treats. Are they tasty? Yes. A good everyday way to kill thirst? Not so much.

Really, kids should hydrate with water and low- or nonfat milk. Even 100-percent juice isn't a great bet. Your child is better off getting fruit from a whole apple than a glass of apple juice. If you decide to serve chocolate milk, make it yourself. You'll be in control of how much fat and sugar is added, which is preferable, since store-bought flavored milk is often high in both.

Do water and milk seem boring? Invest in a charming reusable bottle, and get drinks good and cold before sending them off to school. Other ideas include packing sparkling water or making "spa water" by spiking tap water with citrus or cucumbers.

No matter what your kid's drink of choice, relying on reusable bottles means that fewer plastic bottles, aseptic boxes, and cans end up in the trash heap.

HEY THERE, SWEET STUFF

Sometimes sugar seems hard to avoid. It shows up in everything from sandwich bread to salty snack foods. Overdoing the sweets is hard on kids' teeth and provides empty calories. That said, if your child's diet is largely fresh, whole foods, there's wiggle room for sweets. Here are a few pointers on keeping tabs on sugar and enjoying sweets in moderation:

Read food labels: You may be surprised to see how much sugar is added to something you might consider healthful. Some brands of jarred spaghetti sauce, for example, pack in 1½ tablespoons of sugar in a single serving.

Snack on nature's treats: Opt for foods that are naturally sweet, such as fresh and dried fruit, rather than ones with added sugar, such as fruit roll-ups or heavily sweetened yogurt.

Know sugar's synonyms: Sugar comes in many forms and has many names, including cane sugar, high-fructose corn syrup, dextrose, brown rice syrup, evaporated cane juice, honey, molasses, maple syrup, and agave nectar, just to cite a few.

Sweeten foods yourself: Food manufacturers tend to go overboard with sugar. Adding your own honey, jam, or chopped fruit to plain yogurt, for example, is likely to be a lot lower in sugar than store-bought sweetened yogurt.

Skip the artificial options: If an ingredient was made in a laboratory, it probably doesn't belong in your kid's food. Sugar substitutes such as aspartame, saccharine, acesulfame-K, and sucralose,

along with artificial colors and flavors, should stay where they belong: with the scientists who dreamed them up.

Keep portions petite: A few ounces of low-fat pudding or a little wedge of dark chocolate is enough of a sweet ending, and will allow kids to fill up on sandwiches, fruits, and veggies instead of dessert. Limiting sweets to homemade treats is another option.

Keep Food Cool

One of the major challenges of packing lunch is keeping cold food cold and hot food hot. Perishables can be safely held at room temperature for no more than two hours. Luckily, there are a host of tools and tricks to help keep foods in the safe zone.

Chill out: Use an insulated lunch box along with a freezer pack to maintain safe temperatures for foods such as cheese, deli meats, and yogurt. You can also freeze a reusable water bottle the night before, which can double as an ice pack. (Don't fill it to the tippy-top since liquids expand as they freeze.) Add perishables to lunch boxes just before the kids walk out the door to minimize the amount of time they are out of the fridge.

Hot stuff: A sturdy thermos with a mouth wide enough to fit a spoon is essential to keep foods such as pasta and soup warm and tasting good. Get the food piping hot before filling the container and pop the lid on immediately.

Keep it clean: Food leaking into lunch boxes can be a common occurrence, so clean them with hot soapy water on a regular basis. Packing lunches on supremely clean counters and reminding your kids to wash their hands before meals can also minimize bacteria.

When in doubt, throw it out: Much as it may get under your skin to toss an untouched yogurt, cheese stick, or other perishable that returns home uneaten, it's the safest thing to do. Even with ice packs and thermoses, it's unlikely proper temperatures can be maintained all day long.

Give Lunch a Makeover

Baby steps are the best way to go when it comes to making dietary changes, especially with kids. But even a little change can make a dramatic difference nutritionwise. Here are some examples of simple lunch-box swaps that have a big impact.

THE USUAL	THE UPGRADE	THE UPSIDE
Sliced turkey on white bread, iceberg lettuce, mayo	Turkey on whole-grain pita, hummus, veggies, romaine lettuce	More protein, fiber, folate, iron, and vitamin C
Oil-packed albacore tuna on sour-dough bread, mayo	Chunk light water-packed tuna on whole-grain bread, mayo mixed with nonfat yogurt, spinach	More fiber, iron, and folate; less fat and mercury
Cheese quesadilla on flour tortilla	Quesadilla on whole-wheat tortilla with black beans and sweet potato	More fiber, carotenoids, potassium, and protein; less saturated fat
Honey-roasted nuts	Trail mix with nuts, pumpkin seeds, sunflower seeds, and dried fruits	Greater variety of nutrients, no added sugar, no artificial ingredients, more phytochemicals
Strawberry yogurt, granola bar	Greek yogurt parfait with sliced strawberries, honey, and granola	More protein and vitamin C, less sugar, less packaging, nothing artificial
Three chocolate sandwich cookies	Dark chocolate and whole-grain graham cracker "sandwich"	More fiber and antioxidants, fewer calories, less sugar, no trans fats

About Ingredients

Few ingredients in this book are what I would consider exotic. I am not one to mail-order unusual spices or gourmet foods, so I wouldn't expect you to either. That said, what is familiar to me may be very different from what is familiar to you. Luckily, we live in a time when chain supermarkets regularly stock organic produce and devote entire sections to ethnic foods. I've included details about a couple of less-common ingredients below, and touch on a few other foods worth noting.

LESS-COMMON INGREDIENTS

Agave nectar: A liquid sweetener derived from the agave plant that is less viscous than honey. I prefer light agave for its milder flavor.

Flax meal: Flax meal is nothing more than ground flaxseeds, an ingredient I use to boost fiber and omega-3s in baked goods, smoothies, and hot cereal. The nutrients in flaxseeds are better absorbed when ground rather than whole.

Lavash: A thin Middle Eastern flatbread that's tasty for sandwiches, pizzas, and wraps.

Organic brown rice syrup: A thick liquid sweetener made from brown rice that I use in place of corn syrup.

Sriracha sauce: A spicy chile sauce that adds kick to Asian recipes and is sold in specialty stores, Asian markets, and some supermarkets.

Whole-wheat pastry flour: I've had great success using whole-wheat pastry flour in baked goods that are traditionally made with white flour. It's preferable to standard whole-wheat flour, which is coarser and tends to yield heavier, less delicate cakes, cookies, and muffins.

SALT

I use fine-grain sea salt for most of my cooking. It contains trace minerals, is processed without chemical agents, and is pretty affordable. When I need a generous amount of salt, say for salting pasta water, I reach for my big box of kosher salt.

OILS

I rely on olive oil for my savory cooking, mostly because of its pleasing flavor and nutritional benefits. Look for cold-pressed extra-virgin olive oil to ensure you are getting the maximum quality, health benefits, and taste. For baking I reach for canola oil, which has a milder flavor than olive oil. Seek out organic expeller-pressed canola oil. It's more expensive, but is derived from plants grown without pesticides and is processed without chemicals or heat, all of which can adversely affect the end product.

NUTS AND NUT BUTTERS

Peanut and tree nut allergies are more common than ever. Some schools have a "no peanut" policy, others host a "nut-free" lunch table. I feel for parents who have to work around the challenges and dangers of severe allergies. At the same time, for the great majority of kids, nuts and peanuts can be an enormous source of inexpensive, convenient nutrition. I've included nuts in a number of recipes, both sweet and savory. However, with the exception of one (My Thai Peanut Dip, page 102), nuts, seeds, and nut butters can be used interchangeably to allow for allergies.

DAIRY FOODS

The dairy case is bursting with products that range from the lightest nonfat yogurt to the richest heavy cream. I rely on nonfat and low-fat options when buying milk, yogurt, cottage cheese, and sour cream. For milk, I use 1 percent; for cottage cheese, 2 percent; yogurt, usually nonfat; and sour cream, light. Making these lower-fat choices cuts down on saturated fat and calories, and in some cases, means an increase in the amount of protein and calcium—all with minimal sacrifice in flavor. For families with a milk allergy, lactose intolerance, or who choose not to drink cow's milk, there are loads of nondairy options including soy, almond, rice, and hemp milk. For these alternatives, I always suggest calcium-fortified versions.

When it comes to cheese, however, I nearly always go for the real deal, since the taste of reduced-fat cheese is inferior. I buy high-quality cheeses such as Parmigiano-Reggiano, which are so flavorful that a little goes a long way. I'd rather have one slice of a delicious, nutty, aged Gruyère than two slices of a low-fat look-alike. In the case of cream cheese, I often choose whipped over regular since it's easy for kids to spread and has less saturated fat per tablespoon.

The fat content of the dairy products in my recipes are based on what I use at home. But if you stock something different—say low-fat yogurt instead of nonfat—don't make a special trip to the store. Just use what you have on hand.

About Recipes and Portions

If pulling out measuring cups for a school lunch strikes you as a little unrealistic, I hear you. Luckily, precision is not essential for most recipes, so feel free to riff on what's written and adjust to suit your family. You may want to follow a recipe one time through first, then I'm all in favor of winging it.

You'll notice a range in the number of servings for many of these recipes. This is to take into account different ages and appetites. Even kids who are the same age may eat very differently from one another. My daughter Virginia, for example, has been known to eat breakfast like a lumberjack but has a lighter appetite come lunchtime.

The portions are based on my personal experience as a mom and my expertise as a dietitian. Take them with a grain of salt. As a parent, you know better than anyone what your kid needs. **Your children have their very own, all-natural, built-in guide for what is the right amount of food. It's called an appetite. Invite them to use it, eating when they are hungry, stopping when they've had enough.**

CHAPTER 2

Getting the Job Done

SO NOW YOU KNOW WHAT NEEDS TO GO INTO A SCHOOL LUNCH to make it nourishing, but how do you pull it together without it feeling like your least favorite chore? A little planning and organization can go a long way toward bringing ease to the job. This chapter will serve as a guide on everything from how to stock your pantry to how to keep all those reusable containers clean and ready to go for the next day. You'll also find troubleshooting tips on how to handle it when your kid comes home with his food virtually untouched, as well as the six essential steps to a superb packed lunch.

Fill Your Arsenal

Churning out lunches is aided enormously by a well-stocked and organized pantry, fridge, and freezer. Here's a rundown of what you might find on a good day in my lunch-box larder (fruits and veggies vary by season).

THE CUPBOARD

Assorted fresh fruit, bulk dried and dehydrated fruit, no-sugar fruit leather and applesauce

Assorted nuts and seeds

Nut and seed butters

Crunchy snacks such as popcorn, whole-grain pretzels, and graham crackers

Whole-grain energy bars or granola bars

A bar of good-quality dark chocolate

Canned beans and chickpeas

Boxed, jarred, or canned soups

Canned tuna and salmon

Assorted pastas

Grains such as brown rice and quinoa

Whole-grain bread, bagels, lavash, and/or baguette

Flour and/or corn tortillas

Whole-grain crackers

Brown rice cakes

THE FRIDGE

Low-fat milk, such as cow, soy, and almond milk

Basic condiments, such as mustard, mayo, ketchup, salsa/taco sauce, jam, and light sour cream

Favorite cheeses, such as Cheddar, Monterey Jack, Parmesan, feta, and cottage cheese

A tub of nonfat plain Greek-style yogurt and a tub of nonfat vanilla yogurt

Sliced turkey and other cold cuts

Eggs

Veggies for snacking and salads, such as celery, carrots, bell peppers, cucumbers, fennel, jicama, cherry tomatoes, and snap peas

Salad greens, such as lettuces, spinach, and arugula

Berries, cherries, and other refrigerated fruits

Little extras, such as pickles, cornichons, olives, and roasted peppers

THE FREEZER

Edamame

Peas, corn, and spinach

Organic yogurt tubes

Frozen fruit

Backup loaf of bread

Homemade cookie dough

Flax meal

Frozen homemade soups, beans, and other leftovers

Plan Ahead

To make mornings run more smoothly, take advantage of evenings and weekends to bang out some of the prep.

OVER THE WEEKEND

Restock the pantry.

Wash lunch boxes and containers.

Hard-boil eggs for quick, portable protein.

Make hummus, guacamole, or other veggie dip.

Cook a pot of applesauce.

Wash and dry salad greens.

Roast a couple of chickens—one for that night's dinner, one for lunches. Strip the meat from the bones once cool enough to handle, and store in the fridge for speedy sandwiches, salads, and other mains.

Prepare a few cups of pasta, brown rice, quinoa, or other grains.

Cook a pot of beans.

Bake a batch of granola bars.

THE NIGHT BEFORE

Plan the menu.

Set out clean lunch boxes, napkins, containers, and utensils.

Take advantage of dinner leftovers; pack them into lunch containers as soon as the meal is over.

Pack containers of veggies.

Wash, prep, and refrigerate fruits that won't brown.

Make any sandwiches that hold up well overnight such as PB&Js.

Assemble salads (minus the dressing) in containers and store in the fridge.

Package crunchy sides, goodies, and snacks.

Fill and chill water and milk bottles.

Add a loving touch to the lunch box, such as writing a sweet note or drawing a picture.

THE MORNING OF

Cut apples, pears, and delicate fruits.

Assemble sandwiches and wraps that are best made fresh, such as tuna salad.

Heat soup, leftovers, and other hot foods, and fill thermoses.

Be sure lunch boxes are in the kids' hands before they head out the door!

WHILE YOU'RE AT IT

As long as you're going to the effort to pack your child a wholesome lunch, make one for yourself. It's very little extra work, but a big time- and money-saver come noontime. It's also likely to be more healthful and taste better than what you might pick up on the go.

CHILD LABOR

Yes, you do have laborers. They're called children and they can be very capable lunch packers. Even a preschooler can put trail mix into containers and pull stems off of strawberries, so get them involved early. By middle school they can do the whole job on their own. It may also up the likelihood that they'll actually eat what's packed.

BE A GEARHEAD

It's tempting to pull out the aluminum foil on mornings when you're hunting fruitlessly for the lid that matches the bottom of the little plastic container. But make the effort, because reusable packing supplies protect food better and tread more lightly on the environment. Here's what you'll want to stock:

Insulated lunch boxes to help keep temperatures in the safe zone

Three or four sizes of lidded containers, from teeny ones for sweets, dressings, and condiments to big ones for salads and sandwiches

Reusable sandwich wrappers or bags

Reusable snack bags

Spillproof cups or bottles

Widemouthed thermoses

Reusable or compostable spoons and forks

Cloth napkins

Small freezer packs

Waxed paper bags and parchment paper

A CASE FOR CLOTH

Keep a stack of cloth napkins at the ready to tuck into lunch boxes (not your grandmother's linens—choose ones that won't give you a coronary if they get lost). Consider how many paper napkins (and perhaps a tree or two) this will save over ten-plus years of school lunches.

WASH UP

Sometimes it can feel like all of those reusables are taking over the kitchen, or at the very least, your dishwasher. Consider getting a big bowl of soapy water ready for when your kids arrive home from school. Ask them to empty and rinse their containers and then immerse them in the water. This will help manage the clutter and is also considered preferable by some food safety experts, who suggest washing by hand because the sustained heat of the dishwasher may leach unseemly chemicals from plastic containers.

Troubleshooting

You've packed a healthful lunch and sent it off with your kids to school, but you're not out of the woods yet. Sometimes our best efforts are met with a lukewarm response. Here are some thoughts on what to do when problems arise.

THE BUSY BEE

Plenty of kids claim they have no time for lunch. First, get to the bottom of what's really happening. Is the lunch period too short, or is so much chatting going on that there's no time to eat? Your child's teacher might be able to provide some insight. Ideally, lunch comes after recess, so kids can run off their energy before sitting down. Some schools impose a ten-minute quiet period at the onset of lunch to allow children to focus on food, not each other. Talk to your school about these options, which can make a difference for your child and all kids. Big changes at school aside, make lunches as easy to tackle as possible. For younger children, ensure that containers are a breeze to open.

THE "NO APPETITE" KID

Some children report that they just aren't hungry at lunch. Those are the same ones who often come home crabby and ravenous at the end of the day. Sometimes, a big lunch can be overwhelming, so start by paring it down to small, approachable portions of nutrient-dense essentials. Also, check in to see that they aren't filling up on snacks, sides, and goodies from their lunch-table neighbors.

THE LUNCH TRADER

Lunch envy is nothing new. I still remember yearning for the chips and snack cakes my third-grade friend Stacy brought in each day. But with the time and care you put into a healthful lunch, it's a bummer to hear your kid is swapping it for junky options. Explain why you choose the foods you do and ask your child to stick with the lunch you send. At the same time, leave room for occasional trading—it's important to be flexible.

THE CREATURE OF HABIT

Some kids thrive on routine and want the same lunch every day. This is a tricky one, since eating a variety of foods is important for nutrition. Again, involve your child: Start by taking her to the market with you to pick out new foods. Take baby steps by making small changes over time. Find comfort in the fact that wellness doesn't rest on a single meal, but what's taken in over several days.

THE CHRONIC COMPLAINER

You put a lot of thought into lunch packing and the whining gets old pretty quick. Impose a moratorium on complaining. Instead, put a positive spin on lunch by brainstorming meal ideas with your children. Do a little digging to find out what they like and don't like. Also, get them to pitch in with the packing. It will give them a sense of ownership that may lead to a more upbeat attitude about what's in their lunch box.

THE CHILD WITH A FOOD ALLERGY

Give your child's teacher and school the heads-up about any allergies. Most schools have specific policies in place. Be sure close friends and lunch buddies are aware of the allergies, too.

Six Steps to a Superb School Lunch

1. Start with the main course: The sandwich, salad, or thermos of rice and beans. Be sure you've got some protein in there and tailor portions to your child's age and appetite.

2. Add a fruit: Include cut or whole fruit and do any preparation that will help your child reach for the healthful stuff—peel tangerines, cut melon into bite-size chunks. Aim for seasonal fruit, such as strawberries in spring and grapefruit in winter.

3. Add a vegetable: If your main course is loaded with vegetables, this is optional. Try to mix it up by experimenting with crunchy options such as jicama or fennel. Add a container of salad dressing or other veggie dip to add interest.

4. Include a satisfying side or snack: Kids like crunchy sides and there are plenty of options such as tamari almonds or homemade popcorn (there is more to life than little fish-shaped crackers). Often the side dish becomes a midmorning snack that tides them over until lunch.

5. Don't forget a drink: An icy bottle of water or milk to keep the kiddos hydrated is a lunchbox must, unless those are provided at school, of course.

6. Surprise them with an occasional sweet or loving touch: Goodies (a homemade cookie or dozen chocolate chips) and nonfood "treats" (a note, sticker, or drawing) make lunch something to look forward to.

Mains

When my middle daughter, Rosie, was in kindergarten, she asked me one morning, as she crammed her lunch box into a polka-dotted backpack, "What's my main course today, Mom?"

"Main course?" I asked, thinking, "What five-year-old breaks down her sack lunch into courses?" I wasn't exactly running a four-star restaurant.

But she kind of nailed it. School lunch does have a main course: the turkey sandwich, thermos of leftover spaghetti, or chopped salad. It's the one midday staple that will sustain her through the afternoon if it's the only thing she manages to get down. It's also the perfect vehicle for key nutrients: calcium in the cheese on a sandwich, protein in the beans of a burrito, fiber in a leftover brown rice stir-fry, or vitamin C in a chopped salad.

The recipes in the next handful of chapters are lunch-box mains: sandwiches, salads, wraps, pizzas, and meals reworked from dinner leftovers. All can be knocked out with relative speed and ease, particularly if you've done a bit of legwork ahead of time. Many can be assembled, at least in part, the night before, freeing up your morning to . . . well . . . make other food for your kids, like breakfast.

CHAPTER 3

Stellar Sandwiches

THE SANDWICH IS THE WORKHORSE OF THE SCHOOL LUNCH, which makes sense, since nothing is easier than slapping something tasty between a couple of slices of bread. And while there will always be a place for ham on rye, turkey and Swiss, and other classics, the "same old, same old" gets a little, well, old.

My intention with all of these sandwiches, first off, is to give inspiration and fresh ideas. Beyond that, of course, is good nutrition. Whole grains, beans, and plenty of protein were top of mind when I created these recipes. Fruits or vegetables have been worked into every one, often in ways you might not expect: apple slices tucked into a grilled cheese, and a turkey sandwich layered with four different vegetables. Finally, flavor is essential. There's no better way to get kids to eat their lunches than to make them taste terrific.

Lunch Box Formula for a Stellar Sandwich

1. Choose a *bread* or *flatbread*.
2. Add a *filling*.
3. Include *vegetables* or *fruits* for a nourishing boost.
4. Slather on a tasty *spread*.
5. Mix it up with a *flavorful extra*.

Breads and flatbreads: whole-wheat, multi-grain, rye, pumpernickel, sourdough, sprouted, cinnamon raisin, olive, walnut, rice bread, baguette, ciabatta, focaccia, pita, lavash, naan, tortilla, bagel, bagel thin, bialy, English muffin, hamburger bun

Fillings: beans, chickpeas, lentils, grilled vegetables, chopped raw vegetables, tofu, smoked tofu, tempeh, hard cheeses, soft cheeses, hard-boiled eggs, tuna, shrimp, salmon, smoked salmon, chicken, turkey, ham, prosciutto, salami, mortadella, pork, pastrami, meat loaf, roast beef, steak, lamb

Vegetables and fruits: cucumber, lettuce, cabbage, spinach, arugula, roasted bell pepper, raw bell pepper, carrot, fennel, sprouts, celery, corn, cooked sweet potato, avocado, tomato, grapes, banana, pineapple, pear, apple

Spreads: Dijon mustard, honey mustard, yellow mustard, mayonnaise, cream cheese, hummus, guacamole, tapenade, basil pesto, sun-dried tomato pesto, relish, romesco sauce, barbecue sauce, tartar sauce, ketchup, ranch dressing

Flavorful extras: balsamic vinegar, lemon juice, vinaigrette, soy sauce, sun-dried tomatoes, olives, pickles, capers, pickled onions, olive oil, herbs, spices, anchovies, salt, pepper

HIPPIE-DIPPIE
Bagel Sandwich

THE AVOCADO, sprouts, seeds, and cucumber piled onto this bagel give it sort of a hippie vibe, but you don't have to be a flower child to love it. The combo of flavors and textures is addictive, plus it's loaded with healthful fats that make it nourishing and supersatisfying. The sandwich will serve one hungry kid or two with smaller appetites.

MAKES 1 SANDWICH

1 whole-grain seeded bagel

¼ large ripe avocado

Pinch of salt

1 tablespoon salted roasted sunflower seeds

¼ cup mung bean sprouts

4 thin slices English cucumber

1 thin slice sharp Cheddar cheese, large enough to cover the bagel

1. Slice the bagel in thirds horizontally, reserving the middle slice for another use (see Bagels Slim Down, below).

2. Using a fork, mash the avocado onto the bottom half of the bagel. Sprinkle with the salt and top with the sunflower seeds and bean sprouts, pressing them gently into the avocado so they don't fall off. Lay the cucumber over the sprouts, followed by the cheese. Cap with the remaining bagel top.

3. Cut in half. Wrap well or store in a snug container.

MAKE-AHEAD NOTES: can be made a day ahead and stored in the refrigerator, but best made the morning before school.

TIP: BAGELS SLIM DOWN

Bagels have ballooned over the years, sometimes topping 400 calories apiece, which doesn't leave much room for wholesome fillings. Plus, it's hard for little mouths to get around all that bread. Downsize big bagels by cutting them into three doughnut-shaped slices instead of in half. Take out the middle round and save it for an egg on toast or smeared with peanut butter for a snack. The remaining top and bottom will be plenty for a sandwich.

Smoked Salmon
TEA SANDWICH

I'VE NEVER BEEN ONE to cut the crusts from my kids' bread. "It's a waste," I hear myself saying, just as my own mother did when I was little. Tea sandwiches, such as this delicate, flavorful, smoked salmon one, are the exception, since going crustless is part of the charm. You can always save the crusts for making bread crumbs or feeding birds.

MAKES 1 SANDWICH

2 slices black or pumpernickel bread

2 tablespoons whipped cream cheese

2 teaspoons capers, drained

2 thin slices smoked salmon

6 thin slices English cucumber

1 teaspoon minced fresh dill (optional)

1. Cut the crusts off the bread. Spread both bread slices with cream cheese. Scatter the capers over the cream cheese on one bread slice. Lay the smoked salmon over the capers, followed by the cucumber. Sprinkle with the dill (if using) and top with the remaining bread slice.

2. Cut diagonally into quarters. Wrap well or store in a snug container.

MAKE-AHEAD NOTES: can be made a day ahead and stored in the refrigerator, but best made the morning before school.

Anything Goes
SALAD SANDWICH

CANNED SALMON, chicken, or tuna can all be used for this savory sandwich. You can even turn it into egg salad by replacing the fish or chicken with two chopped hard-boiled eggs along with a generous pinch of salt. I opt for light mayo in most of my cooking, but nothing quite satisfies like the full-fat version in this sandwich.

MAKES 2 SANDWICHES

One 5-ounce can water-packed wild salmon (without skin and bones), chicken, or tuna (see A Tuna Tutorial, page 84), drained

1 stalk celery, finely chopped

1 tablespoon minced fresh dill (optional)

2 teaspoons capers, drained

2 tablespoons finely chopped red onion

2 teaspoons fresh lemon juice

1 tablespoon nonfat plain yogurt

2 tablespoons mayonnaise

4 slices soft whole-wheat bread

2 large crunchy lettuce leaves

1. In a medium bowl, combine the salmon, celery, dill (if using), capers, onion, lemon juice, yogurt, and mayonnaise.

2. Divide the salmon mixture between two of the bread slices, followed by the lettuce. Top with the remaining two bread slices.

3. Cut each sandwich in half. Wrap well or store in snug containers.

MAKE-AHEAD NOTES: the filling can be made a day ahead and stored in the refrigerator; assemble the sandwiches the morning before school.

OH ME, OH MAYO

Some folks take their mayonnaise pretty seriously. I'm a die-hard Best Foods fan (East Coasters know it as Hellmann's); others prefer the Spectrum brand. Plenty of health-minded home cooks never touch the full-fat version, while others think the extra calories are worth every bite. I don't specify what type of mayonnaise to use in my recipes; I leave that up to the cook. Because of the significant fat and calorie savings, I opt for reduced-fat mayo in nearly all of my cooking. One notable exception is a classic tuna sandwich. I gotta go with full-fat mayo for that one, though I try to minimize the impact by swapping yogurt for some of the mayonnaise.

Italian Picnic

SANDWICH

WITH JUST THREE CORE INGREDIENTS—prosciutto, arugula, and balsamic vinegar—this is our family's favorite quick fix for a picnic. Prosciutto is dry-cured Italian ham that is packed with flavor, so a little goes a long way in a sandwich. The arugula, brightened up with the addition of balsamic vinegar, adds a dose of beta-carotene and vitamin C to the mix. If tomatoes are in season, tucking a few slices in the center makes a nice addition.

MAKES 1 SANDWICH

2 thin slices prosciutto

One 4-inch piece baguette, preferably whole-wheat, sliced in half horizontally

⅔ cup loosely packed baby arugula

1 teaspoon balsamic vinegar

1 teaspoon extra-virgin olive oil

1. Pile the prosciutto on the bottom half of the baguette.

2. In a small bowl, toss the arugula with the balsamic vinegar and olive oil. Pile the arugula on top of the prosciutto and drizzle any dressing remaining over it. Top with the remaining baguette half.

3. Wrap well or store in a snug container.

MAKE-AHEAD NOTES: can be made a day ahead and stored in the refrigerator, but best made the morning before school.

Turkey and Veggie

DAGWOOD

DURING GRAD SCHOOL, I studied in a coffee shop where I always ate the same sandwich. It was so tasty that I never strayed. This Turkey and Veggie Dagwood is my interpretation of the original, whereby turkey, Havarti, and artichoke hearts melt together on a seeded baguette and are topped with crunchy vegetables. My kids like the mildly pickled taste of marinated artichoke hearts, which are packed in jars and sold in most supermarkets. This sandwich is excellent hot out of the toaster oven or wrapped up and eaten hours later.

MAKES 1 SANDWICH

2 or 3 thin slices turkey

One 4-inch piece seeded baguette, preferably whole-wheat, sliced in half horizontally

1 marinated artichoke heart, halved

2 thin slices Havarti cheese

4 thin slices English cucumber

4 thin slices red bell pepper

1 large lettuce leaf

½ teaspoon extra-virgin olive oil

1. Preheat the toaster oven or conventional oven to 400°F.

2. Pile the turkey on the bottom half of the baguette. Lay the artichoke on top of the turkey, followed by the cheese.

3. Bake in the oven until the cheese is just melted and the bread lightly toasted, 3 to 4 minutes.

4. Remove from the oven and top the melted cheese with the cucumber, bell pepper, and lettuce. Drizzle the olive oil on the cut side of the remaining baguette half and place on top of the sandwich.

5. Wrap well or store in a snug container.

MAKE-AHEAD NOTES: best made the morning before school.

Turkey and Hummus

CUTIES

MY DAUGHTER VIRGINIA loves everything tiny, so these mini pita sandwiches are right up her alley. If you can't get your hands on little pitas, use half of a regular-size pita. For bigger appetites, increase the recipe by 50 percent, to make three mini sandwiches instead of two.

MAKES 2 MINI SANDWICHES

Two 2- to 3-inch whole-wheat pita breads, each split into 2 halves

1 tablespoon hummus

2 or 3 thin slices turkey

4 thin slices English cucumber

1 crunchy lettuce leaf such as romaine

1. Spread the hummus on the inside of two of the pita rounds. Pile the turkey slices on top of the hummus. Lay the cucumber on the turkey. Tear the lettuce in half and set it on the cucumber. Top each with the remaining pita rounds.

2. Wrap well or store in a snug container.

MAKE-AHEAD NOTES: can be made a day ahead and stored in the refrigerator.

WAFFLE IRON
Grilled Cheese

WE DON'T OWN A PANINI PRESS, but I've found our old-fashioned waffle iron makes a tasty grilled sandwich that holds up in a lunch box, even if it's no longer hot at noontime. The apple adds tartness and crunch, but can easily be left out. If you don't have a waffle iron or a panini press, cook this on the stove top as you would an ordinary grilled cheese. Since it's made in a waffle iron, it only follows that the sandwich doubles as an out-the-door breakfast.

MAKES 1 SANDWICH

⅓ cup coarsely grated Gruyère cheese

2 slices whole-wheat or rye bread

3 thin slices tart apple such as Granny Smith

Oil for the waffle iron

Special equipment

Waffle iron

1. Preheat the waffle iron. While the waffle iron heats up, assemble the sandwich. Sprinkle half of the cheese over one bread slice. Lay the apple slices over the cheese. (There should be enough apple to cover the bread without overlapping.)

2. Top with the remaining cheese and the remaining bread slice.

3. Brush the waffle iron with oil. Put the sandwich in the waffle iron and close tightly. Cook until the bread is browned and the cheese is melted, 2 to 3 minutes.

4. Remove from the waffle iron and let cool for 5 minutes. Cut in half and wrap well or store in a container.

MAKE-AHEAD NOTES: best made the morning before school.

CHICKPEA
Panini

EVEN THOUGH it's a little on the sophisticated side, the Chickpea Panini is one of my daughter Rosie's favorite sandwiches. Chickpeas, lemon, and cumin are a flavorful combo, especially mixed with tangy, creamy goat cheese. As long as you're making this for the kids, be sure to do one up for yourself as well. If you have any leftover chickpea filling, enjoy it spooned onto baguette slices for a satisfying snack.

MAKES 3 SANDWICHES

1 baguette (12 inches or longer), preferably whole-wheat

One 7-ounce can chickpeas (¾ cup), drained and rinsed

1 medium carrot, grated

Juice of ½ lemon

1 tablespoon extra-virgin olive oil

3 dashes of ground cumin

2 ounces fresh goat cheese

1 small handful baby arugula

1. Cut the baguette into three 4-inch segments, reserving any remaining baguette for another use. Cut each segment in half horizontally. If the baguette is particularly thick, scoop a little bread out of the top half and discard.

2. In a medium bowl, use a fork to gently mash the chickpeas, just enough to break them up but not completely pulverize them. Add the carrot, lemon juice, olive oil, and cumin and mix well. Crumble the goat cheese over the chickpeas and mash it into the mixture until the sandwich filling is an even consistency.

3. Spread the chickpea mixture evenly over the bottom halves of the three baguette segments, pressing down gently. Pile the arugula on top of the chickpeas. Top with the remaining baguette halves.

4. Wrap well or store in snug containers.

MAKE-AHEAD NOTES: the filling can be made a day ahead and stored in the refrigerator; assemble the sandwich the morning before school.

DECONSTRUCTED
Caprese

THE DECONSTRUCTED CAPRESE is a sandwich on a skewer, featuring crusty bread, mozzarella cheese, tomatoes, and basil. While it looks sort of fussy, it's actually a snap to pull together and it has a colorful presentation that looks quite smashing in a lunch box. Small mozzarella balls, also known as bocconcini, measure about an inch across and are sold in the specialty cheese section of many supermarkets. Pack the skewers with a little side of olive oil and balsamic vinegar for lunchtime dipping. For bigger appetites, increase the recipe by 50 percent, which will make three skewers instead of two.

MAKES 1 SERVING

6 cherry tomatoes

2 large basil leaves, torn in half

4 small mozzarella balls (bocconcini)

Four 1-inch cubes herbed focaccia bread or crusty Italian bread

Special equipment

Two 10-inch wooden skewers

1. Thread a cherry tomato onto a skewer followed by a piece of basil, a mozzarella ball, and a bread cube. Repeat so that the skewer has two of every item. Add a third cherry tomato on the end of the skewer. Snap the pointed end off the skewer and discard. Repeat with the remaining ingredients.

2. Pack the skewers in a container or wrap them gently in aluminum foil.

MAKE-AHEAD NOTES: can be made a day ahead and stored in the refrigerator.

PB&J Gone Nuts

With supermarket shelves teeming with nut and seed butter options, it's easy to get creative beyond the PB&J. Here are five fresh takes on the classic:

Cashew Butter Banana Roll: Spread cashew nut butter on a whole-wheat tortilla. Top with thin slices of ripe banana. Drizzle with honey, roll up, and cut into rounds.

Peanut Butter Pancakes: Next time you cook pancakes, make two extra ones that are each about 3 inches wide. Spread peanut butter and raspberry jam between them for a supersatisfying pancake sandwich.

Nutty Sushi: Cut the crusts off two slices of whole-wheat bread. Cut the slices in half (lengthwise if the bread is rectangular). Soften the bread by microwaving on high for 10 seconds. Spread a thin layer of almond butter and jam on all four strips of bread. Roll up like sushi and eat with chopsticks.

Apple and Sunflower Butter Dunk: Cut an apple into eight wedges, douse with a squeeze of fresh lemon juice, and store in a container. Spoon 1 to 2 tablespoons of sunflower seed butter in a separate container and scatter 1 teaspoon of roasted sunflower seeds over the top. Send the two items together for dunking.

Carrot Raisin Sammie: Smear peanut or pumpkin seed butter on two slices of whole-grain bread. Scatter one tablespoon of raisins over one bread slice followed by one small grated carrot. Top with the second bread slice. Cut into quarters.

Cold Cuts Crib Sheet

Buying sliced lunch meats can be tricky since so many are processed with loads of salt, sugar, preservatives, monosodium glutamate, coloring, and other additives. Here are a few how-to's on choosing the best cold cuts in the deli case:

Read the label: Look for natural ingredients, and few of them; less is usually more when it comes to food. Choose meat and poultry from animals raised without antibiotics or hormones, something that's a guarantee when you buy organic.

Opt for leaner cuts with less sodium: Fat and salt are often sky-high in packaged cold cuts. Compare labels and go for lower fat and lower sodium options.

Watch the water: Clever manufacturers some-times boost profit margins by pumping water into lunch meats, thereby increasing the weight. You'll know if a product has added water or moisture because the label is required to say so.

Go small: Buy smaller quantities and use them up with relative speed. Meats bought from a deli should be eaten within a couple of days; pre-packaged cold cuts within three to five days of opening.

Know about nitrates: Nitrates are preservatives that lend a distinctively smoky, cured flavor and appealing color to the likes of ham and salami. It's best to watch your intake, which is tricky since labeling can be confusing. Even when marked "uncured" or "no nitrites or nitrates added," meat may indeed have them (albeit from a natural source, such as celery juice). So read the fine print, keep to a moderate portion, and load up on other healthful sandwich fixings.

Cook it yourself: When cooking meat or poultry for dinner, make a little extra for the lunch box. Alternatively, buy cold cuts from a reputable deli. Some even roast and slice their own.

CHAPTER 4

Salads Kids Will Love

SALADS AREN'T JUST FOR GROWN-UPS. If done right, children can be crazy about them. Yet a lot of folks overlook leafy greens for school lunches, thinking they're too complicated or won't get a thumbs-up from the kids. A few elements do have to be in place for successful salads. **1.** They should be crunchy—the fresh bright flavors of chilled cucumber and heart of romaine lettuce will be gobbled with much more enthusiasm than a container of limp greens and baby carrots fished out from the back of the fridge. **2.** They should include kid-pleasing add-ins such as croutons, crumbled cheese, raisins, tortilla chips, and so on. **3.** They should feature a protein-rich food that will provide a bit of heft to the meal—greens and veggies alone won't likely cut it. **4.** They should be packed with care so that salad fixings don't get soggy by the time lunch rolls around.

These six salads fill the bill on all counts, and then some!

Lunch Box Formula for a Salad Kids Will Love

1. Start with 1 cup of *greens*.
2. Add ¼ to ½ cup chopped or sliced *protein-rich food*.
3. Mix in ¼ to ⅓ cup chopped or sliced *vegetables and/or fruits*.
4. Sprinkle 1 to 2 tablespoons *little extras* on top.
5. Fill a small container with 1 to 2 tablespoons of a favorite *dressing*.

Greens: lettuces such as romaine, red leaf, butter, spring mix, Little Gem, iceberg; other greens such as frisée, endive, escarole, radicchio, watercress, arugula, spinach, chard, kale, cabbage

Protein-rich foods: beans, chickpeas, lentils, tofu, tempeh, hard-boiled egg, cheese, tuna, shrimp, salmon, chicken, turkey, steak, pork, ham, lamb

Vegetables and fruits: carrot, cucumber, broccoli, bell pepper, sprouts, fennel, tomato, edamame, celery, cauliflower, zucchini, corn, radish, cooked potato, cooked sweet potato, jicama, apple, grapes, tangerine, pear, papaya, berries, pineapple, orange, peach, mango

Little extras: pumpkin seeds, sunflower seeds, tortilla chips, peanuts, olives, raisins, croutons, dried apricots, crumbled bacon, pita chips, dried cranberries, soft cheeses such as goat cheese and feta, firm cheeses such as Cheddar and Swiss, hard cheeses such as Parmesan

Dressings: Italian, honey mustard, Caesar, balsamic vinaigrette, raspberry, Russian, green goddess, chipotle lime, ranch, oil and vinegar

JAR OF
Everyday Vinaigrette

THERE'S NO SHAME in relying on bottled dressing for lunch-box salads. If you do, be sure to have a peek at the label and look for dressings with less preservatives, sugars, and artificial flavors. That said, a homemade vinaigrette is hard to beat and easy to make. With the exception of the Asian Lunch-Box Slaw (page 56), you can use this vinaigrette for any of the salads in this chapter. If the dressing solidifies when refrigerated, let it sit on the counter for a few minutes and then give it a good shake. Feel free to double or triple the recipe to make a generous jar. It will last indefinitely in the fridge.

MAKES ABOUT ½ CUP

1 tablespoon red wine vinegar

1 tablespoon balsamic vinegar

1 teaspoon Dijon mustard

1 teaspoon soy sauce

1 teaspoon water

⅓ cup extra-virgin olive oil

1. Put the red wine vinegar, balsamic vinegar, mustard, soy sauce, water, and olive oil into a small jar. Screw on the lid and shake vigorously until the dressing forms a smooth emulsion, about 20 seconds.

2. Store in the refrigerator.

DON'T BE A DRIP

Nothing will turn a kid off to salad more than having the dressing leak all over his lunch box. Invest in a couple of small leakproof containers and test their worth by filling them with water, putting on the lids, and giving them a vigorous shake to be sure the liquids stay where they should. If in doubt, pack containers inside a resealable plastic bag just to be on the safe side. Remind your child to shake any dressing before adding it to his salad.

KIDDIE
Cobb Salad

THE COBB IS A PROTEIN-PACKED SALAD that will stick with your kids through the school day. This version relies on smoked turkey for the signature flavor that typically comes from bacon. Blue cheese is an optional add-in since its flavor is too strong for a lot of little ones. The assembly is more composed than chopped, which makes it as pretty as it is tasty.

MAKES 2 SALADS

2 cups chopped butter, red leaf, or romaine lettuce

½ cup chopped tomato or 10 cherry tomatoes, halved

½ large ripe avocado, cubed

2 or 3 slices smoked turkey, coarsely chopped

2 hard-boiled eggs (see page 138), peeled and chopped

2 tablespoons crumbled blue cheese (optional)

Dressing

1 teaspoon soy sauce

2 teaspoons balsamic vinegar

4 teaspoons extra-virgin olive oil

1. Divide the lettuce between two large containers. In each container, arrange half the tomato, avocado, turkey, eggs, and blue cheese (if using) in rows on top of the lettuce.

2. To make the dressing, divide the soy sauce, balsamic vinegar, and olive oil between two small containers. Put on the lids and shake well.

MAKE-AHEAD NOTES: the salad and dressing can be made the night before and stored in the refrigerator, but wait until morning to cut and add the avocado. Be sure to give your child instructions for drizzling the dressing over the salad at lunchtime.

TAKEAWAY
Taco Salad

IT'S NO WONDER kids love this recipe; all the yummy fixings of a taco are transformed into a scrumptious salad. I like to select the crunchiest center leaves for this taco salad because it gives the salad great texture. Packaging the dressing and tortilla chips in separate containers keeps everything crisp until it's time to eat.

MAKES 2 SALADS

2 cups chopped romaine lettuce

½ cup cooked corn kernels

⅔ cup chopped raw vegetables (any combo of carrot, jicama, cucumber, red pepper, tomato)

⅓ cup coarsely grated Cheddar cheese

½ cup shredded cooked chicken or cooked black beans, drained and rinsed

8 salted tortilla chips

Dressing

2 teaspoons fresh lime juice

1 tablespoon plus 1 teaspoon extra-virgin olive oil

Dash of your favorite taco sauce

1 teaspoon honey

1 In a medium bowl, mix together the lettuce, corn, raw vegetables, cheese, and chicken. Divide the salad between two containers.

2 Crumble the tortilla chips and divide between two small containers or wax-paper bags.

3 To make the dressing, in a small bowl, whisk together the lime juice, olive oil, taco sauce, and honey. Divide the dressing between two small containers.

MAKE-AHEAD NOTES: can be made a day ahead. Store the salad and dressing in the refrigerator; leave the chips on the counter. Be sure to give your child instructions for tossing the salad with the dressing and tortilla chips at lunchtime.

FATTOUSH
Salad

HAVE YOU EVER HEARD OF *FATTOUSH?* I hadn't until several years ago, when I learned to make this Middle Eastern specialty in which lettuce, vegetables, herbs, and feta are tossed with plenty of toasted pita bread. It's been a staple in my kitchen ever since, including this ever-so-speedy version that goes over well with my kids. I've left out the herbs in the interest of simplicity, but feel free to add chopped fresh mint or basil if you have it on hand. You can use store-bought pita chips, or make your own by cutting whole pitas into eight wedges. Brush lightly with olive oil, sprinkle with salt, and toast in a toaster oven until just crispy but not browned.

MAKES 2 SALADS

2 cups chopped romaine lettuce (the crunchiest leaves)

½ cup chopped English cucumber

10 cherry tomatoes, halved

½ cup cooked chickpeas, drained and rinsed

¼ cup crumbled feta cheese

12 salted whole-grain pita chips

Dressing

2 teaspoons fresh lemon juice

4 teaspoons extra-virgin olive oil

2 dashes of ground cumin

2 pinches of salt

1 In a medium bowl, mix together the lettuce, cucumber, tomatoes, chickpeas, and feta. Divide the salad between two large containers.

2 Crumble the pita chips and divide between two small containers or wax-paper bags.

3 To make the dressing, divide the lemon juice, olive oil, cumin, and salt between two small containers. Put on the lids and shake well.

MAKE-AHEAD NOTES: can be made a day ahead. Store the salad and dressing in the refrigerator; leave the pita chips on the counter. Be sure to give your child instructions for tossing the dressing and pita chips with the salad at lunchtime.

KID-PLEASER
Chicken Caesar

IF LUNCH-BOX GREENS ARE NEW TO YOUR HOUSEHOLD, the chicken Caesar is a pretty comfortable place to start. The croutons and cheese give it extra appeal, the chicken adds plenty of protein, and the creamy dressing has a pleasing lemony tang. I left out the anchovies, which are standard in a Caesar dressing, since most kids aren't too fond of the fishy flavor.

MAKES 2 SALADS

2 cups chopped hearts of romaine lettuce

1 cup chopped or shredded cooked chicken

3 tablespoons coarsely grated Parmesan cheese

⅓ cup Crunchy Croutons (recipe follows) or store-bought

Dressing

1 tablespoon mayonnaise

2 tablespoons extra-virgin olive oil

1 tablespoon fresh lemon juice

Pinch of salt

Freshly ground pepper

1. Divide the lettuce, chicken, and Parmesan between two containers.

2. Divide the croutons between two small containers or wax-paper bags.

3. To make the dressing, in a small bowl, whisk together the mayonnaise, olive oil, lemon juice, salt, and a grind or two of black pepper. Divide the dressing between two small containers.

MAKE-AHEAD NOTES: can be made a day ahead. Store the salad and dressing in the refrigerator; leave the croutons on the counter. Be sure to give your child instructions for tossing the dressing and croutons with the salad at lunchtime.

Crunchy Croutons

Homemade croutons are so easy to make and miles better (and cheaper) than store-bought versions. They're also a good alternative to pretzels and chips as a crunchy snack, particularly if made with whole-grain bread. This recipe will make enough for four lunch-box salads or one dinner salad for a family of four.

MAKES 1 CUP

1 cup bread cubes from a crusty loaf, such as levain, baguette, or Italian (preferably whole-wheat)

2 teaspoons extra-virgin olive oil

Pinch of salt

1. Preheat the oven or toaster oven to 400°F.

2. Put the bread cubes on a baking sheet, all bunched together. Drizzle the olive oil over the bread cubes and toss with your hands until the bread cubes are evenly coated. Sprinkle with the salt and spread out on the baking sheet.

3. Bake until lightly browned, about 8 minutes.

4. Let cool on the baking sheet for 5 minutes. Store the croutons in an airtight container and use within 1 to 2 days.

WHERE'S
Waldorf?

THIS VERY OLD-FASHIONED SALAD is a variation on one my grandmother made when I was a girl. It appeals to my kids just as it did to me. The spinach, hiding under all of the other goodies, may go unnoticed, even as it adds a nice dose of nourishment to the mix. Yogurt is the base for a creamy dressing.

MAKES 2 SALADS

1 heaping tablespoon nonfat plain yogurt

2 teaspoons fresh lemon juice or white wine vinegar

2 teaspoons mayonnaise

1 tablespoon extra-virgin olive oil

Pinch of salt

⅔ cup chopped unpeeled apple

1 stalk celery, chopped

¼ cup raisins

¼ cup chopped walnuts

1 cup chopped cooked chicken

1 cup loosely packed baby spinach

1 In a medium bowl, combine the yogurt, lemon juice, mayonnaise, olive oil, and salt. Add the apple, celery, raisins, walnuts, and chicken and stir until evenly coated with the dressing.

2 Divide the spinach between two containers and top with the chicken salad.

MAKE-AHEAD NOTES: the chicken salad can be made a day ahead and stored in the refrigerator. Assemble the morning before school.

ASIAN
Lunch-Box Slaw

THIS SLAW is a simpler variation on a main-dish salad I make for dinner all the time. The veggies are crunchy, the dressing is a little sweet, and the peanuts are good and salty. Baked or smoked tofu is a flavorful, nutritious ingredient you can find in the refrigerated section of some supermarkets and many specialty ones. Leftover chicken, steak, or pork would all be a tasty substitution. Buying bagged shredded cabbage will cut down on prep time.

MAKES 2 SALADS

2 cups shredded cabbage

½ medium red bell pepper, thinly sliced

2 green onions, white and light green parts only, thinly sliced

2 tablespoons coarsely chopped fresh cilantro

⅔ cup cubed (⅓ inch) baked or smoked tofu, or cooked chicken, steak, or pork

¼ cup salted roasted peanuts or cashews

Dressing

4 teaspoons seasoned rice vinegar

1 teaspoon brown sugar

1 teaspoon soy sauce

1. In a medium bowl, mix together the cabbage, bell pepper, green onions, cilantro, tofu, and peanuts. Divide the salad between two containers.

2. To make the dressing, divide the rice vinegar, brown sugar, and soy sauce between two small containers. Put on the lids and shake vigorously until the sugar dissolves.

MAKE-AHEAD NOTES: can be made a day ahead and stored in the refrigerator. Be sure to give your child instructions for tossing the dressing with the salad at lunchtime.

TIP: SHAKEN, NOT STIRRED

One simple technique for tossing lunch-box salads is to drizzle the dressing over the greens, sprinkle on any toppings, then pop the lid back on to the container. Give the salad a vigorous shake to mix everything together.

CHAPTER 5

Pinwheels, Pizzas, Wraps, and Roll-Ups

THERE WILL FOREVER BE A PLACE in the school lunch for traditional sandwiches. But the bread aisle is packed with many options beyond the standard sliced loaf that are worth exploring. Consider lavash, the Middle Eastern flatbread that can be rolled around practically any filling and sliced into pinwheels, or pita bread, which makes a killer pizza crust with practically no effort. Tortillas open up even more possibilities, from a veggie-stuffed quesadilla to a rolled-up BLT.

One of the upsides of these alternative sandwich wrappers is that they aren't as bulky as bread can be, so the flavors on the inside really come through. Plus, healthful ingredients such as chopped fruits and sliced vegetables are easy to package up into flatbread or tuck into a tortilla. Yum!

THE PERFECT
Date

THE TASTY DUO of cream cheese and dates on a sandwich is an old-fashioned one. Rolling it up in lavash and cutting it into pinwheels makes it more modern. Kids will love the creamy, slightly sweet filling and crunch of the celery so much that the spinach may just go unnoticed. While nourishing, this wrap is a little light in the protein department, so include a protein-rich side such as nuts or yogurt. Feel free to substitute a large, whole-wheat flour tortilla for the lavash.

MAKES 1 OR 2 SERVINGS

1 whole-wheat lavash (7½ by 10 inches)

¼ cup whipped cream cheese

6 medium pitted Medjool dates, finely chopped

1 stalk celery, finely chopped

⅓ cup loosely packed baby spinach

1 Cut the lavash in half crosswise. Spread both halves of lavash with the cream cheese all the way to the edge. Scatter the dates and celery over the cream cheese, pressing down gently. Lay the spinach on top.

2 With the shorter edge of the lavash toward you, roll up the wrap. Repeat with the remaining lavash. Using a serrated knife, cut each roll into four pinwheels.

3 Store the pinwheels in one or two snug containers, or reassemble the log shape and roll in parchment paper, twisting the ends so it looks like a big Tootsie Roll.

MAKE-AHEAD NOTES: can be made a day ahead and stored in the refrigerator, but best made the morning before school.

Peanut Butter
PINWHEELS

THIS PLAYFUL TWIST ON THE CLASSIC PB&J relies on lavash instead of standard sandwich bread. It gets wrapped around peanut butter, chopped apples, and granola, giving the whole thing great flavor, crunch, and plenty of nutrition. Get this into your kids' hands in the morning and it will fill them up for breakfast, too.

MAKES 2 SERVINGS

1 whole-wheat lavash (7½ by 10 inches)

¼ cup natural unsweetened creamy peanut butter or other nut or seed butter

2 teaspoons honey

⅔ cup chopped unpeeled apple

2 tablespoons granola

1. Cut the lavash in half crosswise. Spread both halves of lavash with the peanut butter all the way to the edge. Drizzle with honey and scatter the apple and granola over the peanut butter, pressing down gently.

2. With the shorter edge of the lavash toward you, roll up the wrap. Repeat with the remaining lavash. Using a serrated knife, cut each roll into four pinwheels.

3. Store the pinwheels in snug containers, or reassemble the log shapes and roll in parchment paper, twisting the ends so it looks like two big Tootsie Rolls.

MAKE-AHEAD NOTES: can be made a day ahead and stored in the refrigerator, but best made the morning before school.

A Better Butter

What's the most healthful nut butter for kids? They're all a little different, and they're all good. I usually rotate two or three options for variety of flavor and nutrients. Here are a few things to keep in mind when considering your choices:

Peanuts, tree nuts, and seeds have somewhat different nutritional profiles, but all have benefits. Almonds, for example, are high in vitamin E, walnuts are a good source of omega-3 fatty acids, and peanuts supply a healthy dose of folate.

All nut and seed butters are rich in both protein and fat, which is one reason to feed them to kids: They are slow to digest and thus can keep hunger at bay.

Keeping less-processed nut butters in the fridge may prevent the oil from separating from the solids. Store jars upside down so you don't have to wade through an oil field when you are ready to make your sandwiches.

Avoid nut butters with either partially hydrogenated oil (a source of trans fat) or fully hydrogenated oil or palm oil (a source of saturated fat). Also, keep an eye out for added sugars. Even nut butters marked "natural" sometimes contain sweeteners, so read the label carefully.

Consider organic options, particularly when it comes to peanut butter, which can be high in pesticide residues.

While most of the fat in nut butters is the "good" kind (i.e., unsaturated), it does make them calorically dense, roughly 90 to 100 calories a tablespoon. So enjoy, but keep portions in check.

Bento a Go-Go

Although the bento box has been around for centuries in Japan, it's relatively new to the United States. This clever approach to packing lunch, whereby different foods are arranged in a compartmentalized box, lends itself to endless variations. See page 150 for a list of favorite bento-style containers. Here are six ideas for lunch-box bentos created around ethnic themes.

The Classic: Japanese flavors such as vegetarian sushi, edamame, seasoned seaweed, Asian pears, Zen snack mix

Tapas Style: Lunch with a Spanish accent, including olives, roasted red peppers wrapped around manchego cheese, serrano ham, Spanish tortilla

Meze: Traditional Turkish fixings such as hummus, pita wedges, feta, tomato and cucumber slices, dried dates, fresh fruit

Ploughman's Lunch: English pub–inspired fare, including a wedge of Cheddar cheese, pickles, hearty whole-wheat roll, apple slices

South of the Border: Mexican favorites such as guacamole, quesadilla, beans, mango with a lime wedge

Parisian: French flavors such as a wedge of Brie, cornichons, baguette slices, grated carrot salad with a Dijon dressing, grapes

BLT
Roll-Ups

BACON HAS SORT OF A NAUGHTY REPUTATION, nutrition-wise at least. But because it's so full of flavor, just two slices are needed to make this wrap a lunch-box fave. The roll-up includes all the standard BLT fixings, plus avocado, which subs in for most of the mayonnaise. It's important to wrap the tomato and avocado inside the lettuce so the tortilla doesn't get soggy.

MAKES 2 SERVINGS

4 slices bacon

2 teaspoons mayonnaise

Two 8-inch whole-wheat flour tortillas

2 large crunchy lettuce leaves

½ large ripe avocado, thinly sliced

2 slices tomato

Pinch of salt

1. Heat a large skillet over medium heat. Put the bacon slices flat in the pan. Cook until the bacon is deeply browned on one side and begins to curl up a bit, about 5 minutes. Using a fork, turn the slices over and cook until the second side is nicely browned and most of the fat is rendered, about 3 minutes. Transfer the bacon to a plate lined with paper towels and let cool for a few minutes.

2. Spread the mayonnaise in a 1-inch-wide strip down the center of each tortilla. Lay the lettuce over the mayonnaise, followed by the avocado. Cut each tomato slice into three strips and lay those over the avocado and sprinkle with the salt. Top each tortilla with two slices of cooked bacon.

3. Roll the ingredients up in each tortilla to form a tight bundle. Cut crosswise in half.

4. Wrap well or store in snug containers.

MAKE-AHEAD NOTES: the bacon can be made a day ahead; assemble the wrap the morning before school.

PESTO
Pita Pizza

I'VE BEEN MAKING PIZZA ON PITA BREAD since I was a teenager, although topping it with pesto and zucchini is a new twist. The result is a tasty and very pretty pie. If your crew isn't especially fond of pesto, swap it out for a couple of tablespoons of marinara sauce instead.

MAKES 2 SERVINGS

One 6-inch whole-wheat pita bread, split into 2 rounds

4 teaspoons pesto

6 small mozzarella balls (bocconcini)

½ small zucchini, very thinly sliced

Pinch of salt

1. Place a rack in the lower third of the oven and preheat the oven or toaster oven to 400°F.

2. Put the pita rounds on a baking sheet and spread the pesto evenly over the inside of each pita with the back of a small spoon.

3. Cut the mozzarella balls into thin slices and lay on top of the pesto, followed by the zucchini and salt.

4. Put the pizzas in the oven and bake until the edges are crispy and the cheese bubbly and beginning to brown, about 7 minutes.

5. Remove the pizzas from the oven and let cool for a few minutes.

6. Cut each pizza into six wedges. Wrap or pack into two containers.

MAKE-AHEAD NOTES: can be made a day ahead and stored in the refrigerator. In the morning before school, pop into the toaster oven to restore crispiness, if you like.

Prosciutto and Arugula

LAVASH PIZZA

LAVASH DOES AN OUTSTANDING JOB as a crust for a crispy pizza. You might be surprised to see Cheddar here instead of the more traditional mozzarella. That's because the first time I made it, sharp Cheddar was all I had in the fridge. Turns out, its tangy flavor works like magic when combined with prosciutto and arugula. I make this pizza for dinner when I'm short on time and ingredients. Consider doubling the recipe; extra slices are handy for snacks or even quick breakfasts.

MAKES 3 OR 4 SERVINGS

2 whole-wheat lavashes (7½ by 10 inches)

⅓ cup tomato sauce

1 cup coarsely grated sharp Cheddar cheese

2 thin slices prosciutto

2 handfuls baby arugula

1. Place a rack in the lower third of the oven and preheat to 450°F.

2. Put the lavashes on a baking sheet and spread the tomato sauce evenly over each lavash with the back of a large spoon. Sprinkle the cheese over the tomato sauce. Tear the prosciutto slices into four or five pieces each and lay on top of the cheese, followed by the arugula.

3. Put the pizzas in the oven and bake until the edges are crispy and the pizzas are no longer floppy when you lift up a corner with a spatula, 10 to 11 minutes.

4. Remove the pizzas from the oven and let cool for a few minutes.

5. Cut each pizza into six rectangular slices. Wrap or pack into storage containers.

MAKE-AHEAD NOTES: can be made a day ahead and stored in the refrigerator. In the morning before school, pop into the toaster oven to restore crispness, if you like.

SWEETIE PIE
Quesadilla

I'VE BEEN MAKING CHILI with black beans and sweet potatoes for years. This takes those two winning flavors and pairs them with melted Monterey Jack cheese for a quesadilla that is far more satisfying than the norm. Cooking the quesadilla over medium instead of high heat allows the sweet potato to get tender by the time the outside is crispy and the cheese is melted. Leftover cooked vegetables such as broccoli, zucchini, or peppers can be chopped up and substituted for the sweet potato.

MAKES 2 SERVINGS

¾ cup coarsely grated Monterey Jack cheese

Two 8-inch whole-wheat flour tortillas

½ cup grated peeled raw sweet potato

¼ cup cooked black beans, drained

2 tablespoons mild green taco sauce

1 teaspoon extra-virgin olive oil

1. Sprinkle half of the cheese evenly over one tortilla. Scatter the sweet potato over the cheese, followed by the beans. Spoon the taco sauce over the beans and top with the remaining cheese and the remaining tortilla.

2. In a medium skillet, heat the olive oil over medium heat. Put the quesadilla in the pan and cook until golden brown and crispy, 2 to 3 minutes. With a spatula, flip the quesadilla and cook until the second side is golden brown and crispy, about 2 minutes.

3. Transfer the quesadilla to a cutting board and let cool for a few minutes.

4. Cut into quarters. Wrap or pack into two containers.

MAKE-AHEAD NOTES: can be made a day ahead and stored in the refrigerator. In the morning before school, reheat in a pan or pop into the toaster oven to restore crispiness, if you like.

CHAPTER 6

Leftovers Made Over

THE EASIEST LUNCH-BOX MAIN IS ONE RECYCLED from the night before. Enjoying dinner a second time around is both a time- and money-saver. Plus, so many leftover ingredients can get a fresh new spin with just a few extra minutes in the kitchen. Reheat cooked spaghetti in a miso broth and you have a nourishing soup, or add black beans to last night's rice for a lunch kids will love. You can even plan for leftovers by making more for a meal than you need. Any extras can go straight into lunch boxes before the dinner dishes are even cleaned up. You'll find loads of ideas to use up leftovers in this chapter, including recipes for pasta, grains, chicken, meat, beans, and lentils.

TERIYAKI
Fried Rice

WARM AND NOURISHING, this panfried rice is a brown-bag favorite. The dish starts with a couple of scrambled eggs to which rice, edamame, and seasonings are added. If you happen to be making eggs for breakfast, it's just a few extra steps to make this savory lunch dish. Naturally, brown rice is more nutritious than white. Leftover farro or barley make tasty substitutions.

MAKES 2 TO 3 SERVINGS

2 teaspoons toasted sesame oil

2 eggs, lightly beaten

2 green onions, white and light green parts only, thinly sliced

1½ cups leftover cooked rice

½ cup cooked shelled edamame

1 tablespoon teriyaki sauce

1   In a medium skillet, heat the sesame oil over medium heat. Add the eggs and scramble until just cooked. Add the green onions, cooked rice, edamame, and teriyaki sauce, and cook, stirring often, until everything is warmed through, about 2 minutes.

2   Divide the fried rice between two or three thermoses.

MAKE-AHEAD NOTES: can be made a day ahead and stored in the refrigerator. In the morning before school, warm up and pack into the thermoses.

"TAKE TWO"
Tabbouleh

CLASSIC TABBOULEH is made with bulgur along with loads of chopped parsley. Here, I've scaled back the parsley and boosted other kid favorites: cucumber, cherry tomatoes, and feta cheese. Although not traditional, quinoa and couscous can be used instead of bulgur. If you want to increase the amount of protein, add ⅓ cup cooked chickpeas or lentils to the mix.

MAKES 2 OR 3 SERVINGS

1½ cups leftover cooked bulgur, quinoa, or couscous

¼ cup chopped English cucumber

8 cherry tomatoes, halved

¼ cup minced fresh parsley

¼ cup crumbled feta cheese

1 tablespoon fresh lemon juice

2 teaspoons extra-virgin olive oil

Pinch of salt

1 In a medium bowl, add the bulgur, cucumber, tomatoes, parsley, feta, lemon juice, olive oil, and salt. Stir gently with a fork until the ingredients are evenly distributed.

2 Divide the tabbouleh between two or three containers.

MAKE-AHEAD NOTES: mix together the bulgur, cucumber, tomatoes, parsley, and feta a day ahead. The lemon juice, olive oil, and salt are best added the morning before school. Store in the refrigerator.

Curried Quinoa

WITH TANGERINES AND DRIED CRANBERRIES

WONDERING WHAT TO DO with the quinoa left over from dinner? Here's your answer. This tasty grain salad hits all the right notes: sweetness from the tangerines, tang from the cranberries, and crunch from the almonds. Among grains, quinoa has a high protein content, and the almonds give this dish an added boost. Feel free to swap out the quinoa for couscous.

MAKES 2 OR 3 SERVINGS

2 tangerines, peeled

1⅓ cups leftover cooked quinoa or couscous

¼ cup toasted slivered almonds

¼ cup dried cranberries

1 tablespoon extra-virgin olive oil

2 teaspoons white wine vinegar

½ teaspoon curry powder

Generous pinch of salt

1. Cut the tangerines in half crosswise. You'll have four halves. Set aside one of the halves for its juice. Pull apart the tangerine segments of the three remaining halves and put into a medium bowl.

2. Add the cooked quinoa, almonds, and cranberries to the bowl. Using your hand, squeeze the juice from the remaining tangerine half over the quinoa. Add the olive oil, vinegar, curry powder, and salt, and stir until the ingredients are evenly distributed.

3. Divide the curried quinoa between two or three storage containers.

MAKE-AHEAD NOTES: mix together the tangerines, quinoa, almonds, and cranberries a day ahead. The vinegar, oil, and salt are best added the morning before school. Store in the refrigerator.

LOVE
Salad

YOUR KIDS will *have* to know how much you love them because you feed them nutritious foods like this salad. OK, maybe not. Maybe they'll grumble that you're giving them legumes instead of Lunchables. But after a few bites, it may just win them over. In addition to being over-the-top healthful, this salad is superflexible. You start with chickpeas or lentils (red, brown, green—any kind is fine), add fennel or celery, stir in dried currants or raisins, and add a fragrant hit of fresh mint (if you have it). Kids can eat it straight up, or feel free to pack pitas or sturdy lettuce leaves so they can scoop up the goods.

MAKES 2 OR 3 SERVINGS

1½ cups leftover cooked chickpeas or cooked lentils, drained

¾ cup finely chopped fennel or celery

¼ cup dried currants or raisins

1 tablespoon extra-virgin olive oil

Zest and juice of ½ lemon, plus more if needed

¼ cup crumbled feta cheese

1 tablespoon minced fresh mint (optional)

Pinch of salt

1. In a medium bowl, add the chickpeas, fennel, currants, olive oil, lemon zest and juice, feta, mint (if using), and salt. Stir gently until combined. Taste and add more lemon juice if needed.

2. Divide the salad between two or three containers.

MAKE-AHEAD NOTES: can be made a day ahead and stored in the refrigerator. Taste the morning before school and add more lemon or salt if needed.

"ME SO" HAPPY
Noodle Soup

IF YOU HAVE LEFTOVER NOODLES of virtually any kind—soba, spaghetti, or ramen—this soup takes fewer than 5 minutes to get from the fridge to the thermos. Miso paste, though not a household staple for everyone, is a good ingredient to have on hand since it has myriad uses beyond this soup, and seems to last forever in the fridge. You can find it in organic markets, Asian specialty stores, and many supermarkets.

MAKES 4 SERVINGS

4 cups low-sodium chicken or vegetable broth

3 tablespoons red miso paste

1½ cups coarsely chopped spinach or other dark leafy greens

3 ounces firm tofu, cut into ½-inch cubes

2 cups leftover cooked noodles such as spaghetti, soba, or udon

2 green onions, white and light green parts only, thinly sliced

Dash of soy sauce (optional)

1. In a medium saucepan, whisk together the broth and miso paste over medium heat until smooth. Raise the heat to high and continue cooking until the broth just begins to boil, about 3 minutes. Add the spinach, tofu, and cooked noodles, and cook just until the ingredients are warmed through and the spinach is wilted, about 1 minute.

2. Remove from the heat and add the green onions. Taste and add soy sauce (if desired).

3. Divide the soup between four thermoses.

MAKE-AHEAD NOTES: can be made up to 2 days ahead and stored in the refrigerator. Reheat the morning before school.

SHORTCUT
Chicken Noodle Soup

CHICKEN NOODLE SOUP is a warm and welcome lunch-box main on a chilly day. This quickie rendition may not be exactly grandma's classic, but it's a big improvement over the canned version, not to mention a great way to take advantage of leftovers. Plenty of noodles make it a winner with the kids.

MAKES 4 SERVINGS

4 cups low-sodium chicken broth

1½ cups water

1 bay leaf

2 stalks celery

2 medium carrots

1 cup dried egg noodles

1 cup leftover chopped cooked chicken

1 handful baby spinach

Juice of ½ lemon

Salt and pepper

1. In a medium saucepan over high heat, bring the broth, water, and bay leaf to a boil.

2. Meanwhile, cut the celery and carrots into ⅓-inch-thick slices.

3. Once the broth mixture boils, add the sliced celery and carrots and the egg noodles and cook until the vegetables and noodles are tender, 7 to 8 minutes.

4. Add the chicken, spinach, and lemon juice. Stir and remove from the heat. Season with salt and pepper.

5. Divide the soup between four thermoses.

MAKE-AHEAD NOTES: can be made up to 2 days ahead and stored in the refrigerator or freezer. Reheat the morning before school.

CREAMY
Black Bean Soup

BLACK BEANS, RICH IN PROTEIN AND FIBER, can be whipped into a delicious, satisfying soup in a matter of minutes. Add chili powder, cumin, and lime juice, and you've got a mild south-of-the-border flavor that kids love. This soup is tasty garnished with a couple of tablespoons of grated Monterey Jack cheese, which you can pack in a separate little container if you like.

MAKES 3 OR 4 SERVINGS

2 teaspoons extra-virgin olive oil

1 medium yellow onion, chopped

½ teaspoon chili powder

¼ teaspoon ground cumin

2 dashes of cayenne pepper

3 cups leftover cooked black beans, drained

⅔ cup water

½ teaspoon salt, plus more if needed

1 tablespoon fresh lime juice

⅔ cup light sour cream

1 In a medium saucepan, heat the olive oil over medium-high heat. Add the onion and cook, stirring often, until tender and translucent, 3 to 4 minutes.

2 Add the chili powder, cumin, and cayenne to the pan and stir until the onion is evenly coated with the spices, another minute or so. Add the beans and water and cook until the beans are good and hot, 2 to 3 minutes.

3 Transfer the beans to a blender. Add the ½ teaspoon salt, the lime juice, and sour cream, and blend until smooth, 1 to 2 minutes. Taste and add more salt if needed.

4 Divide the soup between three or four thermoses.

MAKE-AHEAD NOTES: can be made up to 2 days ahead and stored in the refrigerator. Reheat the morning before school.

TIP: HOMEMADE BEAN BACKUP

If you don't have homemade cooked beans on hand, you can substitute canned. One 15-ounce can of beans is about 1½ cups.

EASY CHEESY
Thermos Beans

CHEESY BEANS are a lunch staple on those days when we don't have a lot of food in the house. Whether I'm relying on my own cooked beans or ones from a can, my kids are big fans. And I am, too, since beans are so nutritious. If you like, you can serve this with a little stack of tortilla chips on the side for interest and crunch.

MAKES 2 SERVINGS

1½ cups leftover cooked black or pinto beans, drained

½ cup fresh or frozen corn kernels

3 tablespoons canned diced mild green chiles

Juice of ½ lemon

Salt

½ cup coarsely grated sharp Cheddar or Monterey Jack cheese

1. In a small saucepan, heat the beans, corn, and chiles over medium heat until the corn is fully cooked, about 5 minutes.

2. Squeeze the juice from the lemon half over the bean mixture and season with salt. Remove from the heat, add ¼ cup of the cheese, and stir until combined.

3. Divide the bean mixture between two thermoses. Top with the remaining cheese.

MAKE-AHEAD NOTES: can mix together the beans, corn, and chiles a day before and store in the refrigerator. Reheat the morning before school and add the lemon juice, salt, and cheese.

KICK THE CAN

Most food manufacturers use an unfriendly chemical called BPA (bisphenol A) to line their cans. BPA is best minimized, especially among pregnant women and young children. Luckily, there are options such as buying soups and other foods in glass jars and boxes, or looking for food manufacturers that can without BPAs.

Crock-Pot of Beans

If the only thing I could do with my slow cooker were to cook dried beans, the appliance would still be worth the cost and storage space. Beans are dirt cheap, meganourishing, lunch-box friendly, and better tasting than canned.

This method takes less than 5 minutes of prep, requires no babysitting a bubbling pot, and leaves you with an abundance of beans to use for tacos, soups, salads, and even sandwiches. Store whatever you don't eat after several days in the freezer, where it will keep for up to 3 months.

Rinse and drain 1 pound of dried beans, picking out any stones. Put the beans in the slow cooker and cover with water by 4 inches. Do not turn on the slow cooker. Soak at least 8 hours or up to overnight.

Drain the soaked beans, rinse, and put them back into the slow cooker. Add 2 peeled garlic cloves, 2 bay leaves, and 1 onion that has been peeled and quartered. Cover with water by 1½ inches. Cook on high until just tender,

4 to 4½ hours for black, pinto, and white beans; 5 to 5½ hours for chickpeas. Cooking times will vary depending on your appliance. Remove the bay leaves, any obvious onion or garlic pieces, and season with salt.

Note: This method is not appropriate for cooking kidney beans, which contain phytohemagglutinin, a toxin that may not be eliminated in the slow cooker.

OODLES OF
Sesame Noodles

THIS RECIPE will work with whatever vegetables you have on hand that are good eaten raw. Just chop them up, toss them with leftover noodles, and then coat them with a lip-smacking, Asian-accented peanut sauce. Yum! If peanut butter is off-limits, use cashew butter instead. On days you don't happen to have leftover pasta, look for cooked Asian noodles such as soba and udon in the refrigerated section of your supermarket, usually near the tofu.

MAKES 2 OR 3 SERVINGS

1 tablespoon plus 1 teaspoon toasted sesame oil

1 tablespoon plus 1 teaspoon natural unsweetened creamy peanut butter

1 teaspoon soy sauce

1 tablespoon seasoned rice vinegar

1 teaspoon honey

1 tablespoon water

2 cups leftover cooked noodles such as spaghetti, soba, or udon

½ cup chopped raw crunchy vegetables (any combo of carrots, cucumbers, red peppers, snap peas)

½ cup cubed (⅓ inch) baked tofu or ½ cup cooked shelled edamame

2 green onions, white and light green parts only, thinly sliced

1. In a medium bowl, whisk together the sesame oil, peanut butter, soy sauce, rice vinegar, honey, and water until creamy and smooth.

2. Using tongs, add the cooked noodles to the bowl and toss until evenly coated with the sauce. Add the raw vegetables, tofu, and green onions, and toss again until coated with the sauce and evenly distributed.

3. Divide the sesame noodles between two or three containers.

MAKE-AHEAD NOTES: can be made a day ahead and stored in the refrigerator.

Tuna Pasta
CLASSIC

GROWING UP, this simple cold pasta was a meal my mom made for supper that sometimes landed in our lunch boxes the next day. The humble combination of tuna, pasta, and mayo is the ultimate comfort food. Best of all, it calls for ingredients that are likely already in your pantry.

MAKES 3 SERVINGS

One 3-ounce can water-packed tuna, drained

1 medium carrot, finely chopped

1 stalk celery, finely chopped

2 tablespoons finely chopped red onion

1½ cups leftover cooked short pasta such as penne or rotini

1 tablespoon fresh lemon juice

2 to 3 tablespoons mayonnaise

1 In a medium bowl, break up the tuna with a fork. Add the carrot, celery, onion, and cooked pasta, and stir until combined.

2 Add the lemon juice and 2 tablespoons of the mayonnaise. Stir until combined. Taste and add more mayonnaise if needed.

3 Divide the tuna pasta between three containers.

MAKE-AHEAD NOTES: can be made a day ahead and stored in the refrigerator.

A Tuna Tutorial

Canned tuna is convenient, low in saturated fat, and a good source of protein. The problem is, tuna can also be high in something you don't want—the environmental pollutant mercury. To keep mercury levels in check, be smart about the kind of tuna you choose and how much you feed your family. Here are a few pointers to help you shop wisely:

Buy water-packed chunk light tuna, which has the lowest level of mercury of any variety. This is not to be confused with chunk white tuna or albacore, which tend to be high in mercury and are best avoided.

Alternatively, look for albacore labeled "pole caught," which means the fish are smaller than the conventional variety, with less mercury buildup.

Turn to the experts at the Natural Resources Defense Counsel for guidelines on how much canned tuna is safe for kids based on their body weight. The guidelines can be found at www.nrdc.org/health/effects/mercury/tuna.asp.

Consider using canned wild Alaskan sockeye salmon instead of tuna. It's rich in omega-3s, low in mercury, and sustainably caught. It's got a fairly strong flavor, so consider mixing in equal parts canned chicken when you introduce it to your kids. They may take to it better this way.

CHINESE
Tacos

ON ONE OF OUR FIRST DATES, my husband introduced me to minced squab in lettuce cups, the specialty of the house at his favorite Chinese restaurant. Ever since, I've been hooked. This is a supersimplified spin on that famous dish. Kids really respond to the sauce's soy and hoisin flavors and all the crunchy bits of the filling—cucumbers, cashews, and sprouts. Pack it up by storing the filling in one container and the lettuce in another, all to be assembled like little tacos at the lunch table.

MAKES 2 SERVINGS

1 tablespoon plus 1 teaspoon hoisin sauce

1 teaspoon soy sauce

1 tablespoon seasoned rice vinegar

1 cup leftover chopped cooked chicken, beef, or pork

½ cup coarsely chopped mung bean sprouts

¼ cup finely chopped English cucumber

2 tablespoons chopped roasted cashews

4 medium crunchy Boston or Bibb lettuce leaves

1. In a medium bowl, whisk together the hoisin sauce, soy sauce, and rice vinegar.

2. Add the chicken, bean sprouts, cucumber, and cashews, and stir until the ingredients are evenly coated with the sauce.

3. Divide the chicken mixture between two containers and pack the lettuce in two other containers.

MAKE-AHEAD NOTES: can be made a day ahead and stored in the refrigerator. Be sure to give your child instructions for spooning the filling onto the lettuce leaves at lunchtime.

BBQ
ON A BUN

SHREDDED CHICKEN, BEEF, OR PORK slathered in barbecue sauce and served on a soft bun: What's not to like? The wholesomeness of the whole-wheat bun and shredded cabbage hardly register with the kiddos with all the other deliciousness going on. Dads (at least the one in our household) are particularly fond of this as well.

MAKES 2 GENEROUS SERVINGS; ½ SANDWICH WILL SUFFICE FOR SMALLER APPETITES

---

1 heaping cup leftover shredded cooked chicken, beef, or pork

¼ cup favorite barbecue sauce

2 soft whole-wheat hamburger buns

2 teaspoons mayonnaise

⅔ cup shredded cabbage

1 Put the chicken into a small saucepan. Pour the barbecue sauce over the chicken and stir until evenly coated. Over medium heat, cook, stirring often, until piping hot, 2 to 3 minutes. Divide the chicken mixture between two thermoses.

2 While the chicken mixture heats up, spread the tops of the buns with mayonnaise and pile the cabbage on the bottoms. Sandwich the bottoms and tops of the buns together, and wrap well or store in snug containers.

MAKE-AHEAD NOTES: can shred the cabbage and prep the chicken mixture the night before. Reheat and prepare the buns the morning before school. Be sure to give your child instructions for spooning the barbecue onto the buns at lunchtime.

Ten Dinners That Make Great Leftovers

Sometimes supper transforms easily into lunch-box leftovers. Here are ten no-brainers to set aside for the next day:

1. Chicken Drumsticks: Wrap a napkin around the leg to keep things tidy.

2. Chili: Pack with a little stack of tortilla chips or crackers to do the scooping.

3. Kebab: Pull the fixings off the skewer and tuck into a pita pocket along with a side of plain yogurt or salad dressing to drizzle on at the lunch table.

4. Pasta: Dribble a little water over leftover pasta to moisten any sauce that's been absorbed, and then reheat well and store in a thermos.

5. Meat Loaf: Slice and serve between a couple of pieces of whole-wheat bread with a squirt from the ketchup bottle.

6. Homemade Soup: Consider every variety of soup suitable for leftovers; pack with a container of crackers or croutons for added crunch.

7. Grilled Veggies: Stack them inside a split baguette with a smear of goat cheese for a sophisticated and healthful meal.

8. Pizza: Pack warm or cold, homemade or from a pizza parlor.

9. Chicken Parmesan: Cut into "finger"-size portions and accompany with a little container of marinara sauce for dipping.

10. Mexican Entrées: Heat up leftover enchiladas, tamales, or burritos and keep warm in a thermos.

Sides

You've managed to pull together a splendid lunch-box main. Congrats. Now it's time to move on to sides: all the extras that fill in the gaps both nutritionally and tastewise. Snacks are an important bridge between meals and another chance to pack in some nourishment. If your main course comes up short on protein, calcium, or other nutrients, for example, sides can lend a boost.

Because sides are smaller than mains, they're perfect for taking advantage of the bits and bobs in the fridge and pantry: the last tangerine in the fruit bowl, the steamed broccoli left over from dinner, the few remaining whole-grain crackers.

The variety and volume of sides is up to you, since every child is different. My kids think something has gone terribly wrong if fewer than three items show up in their lunch boxes. Others find too many little containers overwhelming. Use your judgment to determine portions and variety, and check out what comes home at the end of the school day. Containers licked clean or packed full are your best guide.

CHAPTER 7

Fruit and Veggie Sides

NOTHING BRIGHTENS A LUNCH BOX quite like fruits and vegetables. They add bold colors, rich textures, and refreshing flavors, not to mention vitamins, minerals, phytochemicals, and fiber. The USDA now recommends half of every plate at every meal be filled with fruits and veggies. If you can include a serving of both at lunch, you're off to a great start.

Often fruits and veggies are a lunch-box afterthought, but making them a priority pays off, especially since most kids are more apt to reach for cheese and crackers than cherry tomatoes. Pack mega-appealing options—a juicy, easy-to-peel satsuma tangerine at the season's peak or a bundle of tender young carrots with a crock of homemade ranch dressing—and your child will have a harder time passing them by. Make produce important and you may start to see lunch containers come home just how you want them: completely empty.

I HEART
Watermelon

NOT FOR EVERY DAY, but when the mood strikes, juicy, heart-shaped watermelon is a pretty darling way to say "I love you" in a lunch box. Plus, even though it seems a little fussy to be pulling out cookie cutters on a weekday morning, it adds mere seconds to lunch prep. If you're not usually given to these sorts of kitchen crafts, your kids will think you're a genius.

MAKES 1 OR 2 SERVINGS

One ¾-inch-thick slice seedless watermelon

Special equipment

Heart-shaped cookie cutter

1. Set the watermelon slice on a cutting board (be sure it's not a board that was just used to cut garlic!).

2. Press the cookie cutter into the watermelon, cutting out as many hearts as you can fit in the slice. If you don't have a heart-shaped cookie cutter, use a paring knife to cut your own rustic hearts.

3. Pack into one or two containers.

MAKE-AHEAD NOTES: can be made a day ahead and stored in the refrigerator.

HONEY-LIME
Melon

RIPE CANTALOUPE is pretty terrific all on its own: sweet as candy, rich in beta-carotene, high in potassium, and low in calories. A drizzle of honey and a squeeze of lime puts it over the top. My oldest daughter, Isabelle, likes to get fancy with this one by using a melon baller to scoop the flesh from the rind. You can substitute mango or papaya for the cantaloupe, figuring that you'll need about 2½ cups of fruit.

MAKES 4 SERVINGS

½ cantaloupe, seeded

1 lime, quartered

2 teaspoons minced fresh mint

2 teaspoons honey

Ⓐ Put the cantaloupe cut-side down on a cutting board. Use a sharp knife to shear off the rind, exposing the orange flesh. Cut the cantaloupe into ¾-inch cubes.

Ⓑ Divide the cantaloupe cubes between four containers. Squeeze a lime quarter over the fruit in each container, then sprinkle the mint on top, followed by the honey. Put on the lids and give each one a gentle shake so the melon is evenly coated with the other ingredients.

MAKE-AHEAD NOTES: can be made a day ahead and stored in the refrigerator, but best made the morning before school.

VERY
Berry Skewers

THE BEAUTY OF BERRIES is that they're not only an easy sell with kids who seem to gobble them down like lollipops, they're also a good source of vitamins, fiber, and antioxidants. As a mom, I love that. When the first berries start to show up in farmers' markets toward the end of the school year, threading them onto skewers is a colorful way to pack them in a lunch. Kids will enjoy making these with you, although the delicate fruits demand a gentle hand.

MAKES 2 SERVINGS

4 medium strawberries, stemmed and halved

⅓ cup blueberries, raspberries, and/or blackberries

Special equipment

Four 6-inch wooden skewers

1. Thread a strawberry half onto a skewer followed by a blueberry, raspberry, and/or blackberry. Repeat until each skewer is filled, alternating the different berries. Snap the pointed ends off the skewers and discard.

2. Pack two skewers in each of two containers or wrap them gently in aluminum foil.

MAKE-AHEAD NOTES: can be made a day ahead and stored in the refrigerator.

PRECIOUS CARGO

Protect tender fruits such as peaches and pears from getting mushy come lunchtime by storing them whole in individual containers. Tucking a small cloth around the fruit can protect it further and double as a napkin.

TEENSY
Tropical Salad

THIS SALAD is all about texture: tender fresh fruits combined with crispy coconut flakes and chewy dried mango. By cutting all the ingredients small, the flavors come through in every bite. Pair with a container of plain or lightly sweetened yogurt to turn this side into a main. Go übertropical and add a couple of tablespoons of chopped macadamia nuts to the mix.

MAKES 3 OR 4 SERVINGS

1 medium fresh mango, cut into ½-inch cubes

⅓ medium pineapple, cut into ½-inch cubes

¼ cup unsweetened coconut flakes

¼ cup finely chopped unsweetened dried mango

½ teaspoon vanilla extract

1. In a small bowl, add the fresh mango, pineapple, coconut flakes, dried mango, and vanilla and stir until combined.

2. Pack into three or four small containers.

MAKE-AHEAD NOTES: can be made a day ahead and stored in the refrigerator.

LOOKS DO MATTER

Some fruits, particularly apples and pears, begin to brown the moment they're cut, which is off-putting enough that some kids will steer clear even if the flavors are exactly the same. Minimize color changes by squeezing a little fresh lemon juice over the flesh of the sliced fruit before packing it into containers.

WINTER
Jewel Box Salad

THE PINK-RED HUE OF POMEGRANATE SEEDS reminds me of gorgeous little gems. Pairing this fruit with something more common, like tangerines, may help ease the introduction of this less familiar fruit. Since extracting pomegranate seeds can be messy and a little tricky, immersing them in water while you work helps enormously (see "Getting Out Those Tiny Seeds," below). Invite your kids to pitch in; they might relish the challenge. Any leftover pomegranate seeds are great for snacks, added to salads, or sprinkled over yogurt.

MAKES 3 SERVINGS

2 tangerines, peeled

1 large ripe kiwi

½ cup pomegranate seeds

1 teaspoon minced fresh mint (optional)

1. Cut the tangerines crosswise into ½-inch-thick slices. Pull apart all the ½-inch-thick segments and put in a medium bowl.

2. With a sharp paring knife, peel the kiwi and cut into ⅓-inch cubes. Add to the bowl with the tangerines, along with the pomegranate seeds and mint (if using). Stir until combined. Pack into three containers.

MAKE-AHEAD NOTES: can be made a day ahead and stored in the refrigerator.

GETTING OUT THOSE TINY SEEDS

Extracting pomegranate seeds is easy once you get the hang of it. Start by cutting the fruit into quarters through the stem end. Consider donning an apron since the juice can stain.

Immerse the fruit quarters in a large bowl of water. Using your hands, pry the sections apart with your thumbs to dislodge the seeds. The seeds will settle to the bottom of the bowl and the pale membrane that encases them will float to the top. Scoop up the membrane and discard. Drain the seeds and store in the fridge until ready to use.

JUICE BOX
Applesauce

THIS APPLESAUCE IS SO EASY, I sometimes make it in the morning before school. The peels are left in the sauce to boost the fiber and cut down on labor (no peeling necessary). Having an apple slicer will make it go that much quicker. When the applesauce has cooled, spoon it into small containers and store in the fridge for grab-and-go snacks. Relying on reusables is more economical and earth-friendly than buying prepackaged single-serve applesauce.

MAKES ABOUT 4 ½ CUPS; 9 SERVINGS

8 medium Granny Smith, Pink Lady, or other favorite cooking apple

One 6.75-ounce apple juice box (about ¾ cup juice)

2 tablespoons pure maple syrup

1 teaspoon ground cinnamon

1. Use an apple slicer to cut the apples into wedges and remove the cores. If you don't have an apple slicer, use a paring knife to cut apples into 1-inch-wide wedges and remove the cores.

2. In a large pot, add the apples, apple juice, maple syrup, and cinnamon. Cook over high heat, giving everything a good stir, until the liquid comes to a boil. Reduce to a simmer and cover with a lid.

3. After 15 minutes, stir the apples, re-cover, and continue to simmer until the apples are tender enough to easily mash with a fork, 20 to 30 minutes. (The time will vary depending on the variety of apple and cooking temperature.)

4. Remove from the heat and mash into a chunky sauce using a big fork or potato masher. Let the applesauce cool.

5. Spoon the applesauce into a bowl or container, cover, and refrigerate. Pack into small containers as needed for lunches.

MAKE-AHEAD NOTES: can be made up to 1 week ahead and stored in the refrigerator.

Really Ranch Dip

WITH VEGGIES IN THE RAW

THIS IS A MORE HEALTHFUL SWAP for bottled ranch dressing, which is often made with artificial flavors and MSG. My kids maintain that mine is better than store-bought, which I consider an honor since they're crazy for the bottled stuff. You can turn this from dip to dressing by adding a splash of milk. For a milder flavor, cut the amount of garlic in half.

MAKES ABOUT ¾ CUP; 2 TABLESPOONS PER SERVING

½ cup nonfat plain yogurt

⅓ cup light sour cream

2 tablespoons mayonnaise

2 tablespoons minced fresh chives

1 small garlic clove

1 teaspoon white wine vinegar

1 tablespoon extra-virgin olive oil

¼ teaspoon salt

Chopped or sliced raw vegetables for dipping (such as broccoli, cherry tomatoes, fennel)

1. Put the yogurt, sour cream, mayonnaise, chives, garlic, vinegar, olive oil, and salt in the bowl of a food processor fitted with a metal blade. Process until smooth, about 30 seconds.

   (If you don't have a food processor, mince the garlic with a knife. In a medium bowl, whisk together the garlic with the remaining ingredients until smooth.)

2. Keep the dip in the fridge in a covered bowl or storage container. When ready to use, pack the dip and vegetables in separate containers.

MAKE-AHEAD NOTES: can be made up to 4 days ahead and stored in the refrigerator.

"When you choose organics, you are voting with your fork for a planet with fewer pesticides, richer soil, and cleaner water supplies—all better in the long run. When you choose locally grown produce, you are voting for conservation of fuel resources and the economic viability of local communities, along with freshness and better taste."

——MARION NESTLE

My Thai Peanut Dip

WITH GARDEN-FRESH FAVES

GETTING PEANUT BUTTER–LOVING KIDS TO EAT their vegetables is easy with this addictive dip. It's so tasty, I always squirrel a little away for myself before it goes into the lunch boxes. If your kids go to a "peanut-free" school, save this one for an after-school snack.

MAKES ABOUT ⅔ CUP; 2 TABLESPOONS PER SERVING

⅓ cup natural unsweetened creamy peanut butter

¼ cup water

1 ½ teaspoons soy sauce

2 teaspoons honey

2 tablespoons fresh lime juice

1 small garlic clove

Dash of Sriracha or other chile sauce (optional)

Chopped or sliced raw vegetables for dipping (such as snap peas, cucumbers, bell peppers)

1. Put the peanut butter, water, soy sauce, honey, lime juice, and garlic in the bowl of food processor fitted with a metal blade. Process until smooth, about 30 seconds.

2. Add a dash of Sriracha (if using). Process for a few seconds until blended.

   (If you don't have a food processor, mince the garlic with a knife. In a medium bowl, whisk together the garlic with the remaining ingredients until smooth.)

3. Keep the dip in the fridge in a covered bowl or storage container. When ready to use, pack the dip and vegetables in separate containers.

MAKE-AHEAD NOTES: can be made up to 5 days ahead and stored in the refrigerator.

Guacamole

AND CRUNCHY CRUDITÉS

THIS GUACAMOLE IS STRIPPED DOWN to its best parts—avocado, lime, onion, and salt—yet it's every bit as appetizing as the fancied-up versions with cilantro, chiles, sour cream, and so forth. The "healthful" fats in avocado fill up your kids as well as aiding the absorption of nutrients in the vegetables that go along with it. Now that's a superfood!

MAKES ABOUT ⅔ CUP; 3½ TABLESPOONS PER SERVING

1 medium ripe Hass avocado, peeled, halved, and pitted

2 teaspoons fresh lime juice

1 tablespoon finely chopped red onion

Pinch of salt, plus more if needed

Chopped or sliced raw vegetables for dipping (such as jicama, cucumbers, carrots)

1 In a medium bowl, add the avocado, lime juice, red onion, and salt and mash with a fork until smooth enough for your liking. Taste and add more salt if needed.

2 Keep the guacamole in a small bowl. Lay plastic wrap directly on the surface of the guacamole to minimize browning. When ready to use, pack the dip and vegetables in separate containers.

MAKE-AHEAD NOTES: can be made a day ahead and stored in the refrigerator.

Hummus with a Twist

AND VEGGIES TO DIP

HUMMUS IS A NOURISHING SPREAD that's now as common as cream cheese in school lunches. In this version, I've added a roasted sweet potato, which makes it a touch sweet, super-creamy, and packs an antioxidant punch, all changes that will likely go under the radar with most kids. If you don't have tahini—Middle Eastern sesame paste—you can leave it out and still end up with a tasty result. Just drizzle in a little more olive oil.

MAKES ABOUT 2 CUPS; ¼ CUP PER SERVING

1 small sweet potato

1½ cups cooked chickpeas, drained

2 tablespoons tahini

2 tablespoons extra-virgin olive oil

Juice of 1 lemon

1 small garlic clove

¼ cup water plus more if needed

½ teaspoon ground cumin

½ teaspoon salt

Chopped or sliced raw vegetables for dipping (such as bell peppers, fennel, and carrots)

1. Preheat the oven or toaster oven to 400°F.

2. With the tip of a knife, pierce the sweet potato a few times and put on a baking sheet. Bake until tender enough to mash with a fork, 40 to 45 minutes.

3. When cool enough to handle, peel the skin off the sweet potato with your hands.

4. Put the flesh of the sweet potato in the bowl of a food processor fitted with a metal blade. Add the chickpeas, tahini, olive oil, lemon juice, garlic, water, cumin, and salt, and process until smooth, 1 to 2 minutes. Add more water if the hummus seems too thick. Process for a few seconds until blended.

5. Keep the hummus in the fridge in a covered bowl or storage container. When ready to use, pack the dip and vegetables in separate containers.

MAKE-AHEAD NOTES: can be made up to 1 week ahead and stored in the refrigerator or freezer. Taste and add lemon juice and/or olive oil to defrosted hummus if needed.

Getting In Those Greens

There's nothing wrong with the abundance of baby carrots in school lunches these days, but there is a wide world of vegetables out there beyond bags of bite-size bunny food. Here are ten ideas to get your kids asking for seconds:

1. Douse sliced cucumbers or another crunchy vegetable with seasoned rice vinegar.

2. Add a squeeze of lime and a dash of chili powder to jicama sticks.

3. Pack roasted or blanched broccoli, Brussels sprouts, or cauliflower with a wedge of lemon or a sprinkle of grated cheese, or both.

4. Tuck a pat of butter in the center of a warm, cooked sweet potato and pack in a thermos.

5. Grate a carrot, add a spoonful of raisins, a pinch each of salt and sugar, and toss with a splash of white wine vinegar.

6. Skewer bite-size vegetables and pack with a container of salad dressing for dipping.

7. Combine vegetables and fruits in the same container: apple slices with carrot coins, cucumber slices with halved grapes, Asian pear chunks with fennel slices.

8. Save those little packets of takeout soy sauce and tuck them alongside leftover cooked veggies.

9. Toss a small handful of any of the following into soups, stews, and pastas: leftover chopped vegetables, spinach, arugula, corn, or peas.

10. Include your child's favorite dip or sauce when you pack vegetable crudités: salad dressing, hummus, teriyaki sauce, peanut sauce, or barbecue sauce. The four veggie dips in this chapter are a great place to start.

Lunch Box–Friendly Fruits and Vegetables by Season

It's easy to fall into a school-lunch rut, packing the same rotation of apple and celery sticks day in, day out. Mix it up by incorporating something new from the produce aisle, whether as part of a salad, sliced as a side, or worked into a thermos of soup.

Here are some fresh ideas for fruits and vegetables, listed by season. Keep in mind that many cross over from one season into the next and seasonal produce may vary depending on where you live.

WINTER	SPRING	SUMMER	FALL
Mandarins	Kumquats	Peaches	Kiwis
Tangelos	Strawberries	Apricots	Asian Pears
Grapefruits	Cherries	Plums	Apples
Navel oranges	Cherry tomatoes	Melons	Pomegranates
Blood oranges	Asparagus	Nectarines	Persimmons
Fennel	Peas	Green beans	Grapes
Sweet potatoes	Carrots	Cucumbers	Bell peppers
Cabbage	Snap peas	Corn	Hass avocados
Kale	Beets	Tomatoes	Eggplants
Brussels sprouts	Radishes	Figs	Blackberries

Comparing Fresh, Frozen, and Canned

Fruit comes in many forms, ranging from bare naked off-the-vine to heavily processed, and thus varies considerably in flavor, texture, and nutritional value. Here's my take on what matters most when it comes to choosing fruit.

Fresh first: Megafresh, locally grown, seasonal fruit is hard to beat both for flavor and nutrition. One of the best ways to get your hands on excellent fruit is to visit the farmers' market so you can sample the wares and perhaps be lucky enough to buy food picked that very same day.

Frozen, too: When fruit is frozen, it's usually done at the peak of ripeness and soon after harvesting, which preserves the nutritional value. Some fruits fair better frozen than others and can go from the freezer right into the lunch box. They're already washed, prepped, and cut and will defrost by the time lunch rolls around. Our faves include blueberries, raspberries, mango, and pineapple.

Canned on hand: Fruits preserved in cans and jars aren't as good for you as fresh or frozen because the processing eliminates some nutrients. But having a small supply in the pantry can be a handy backup, especially preserved applesauce, peaches, and pineapple, which hold up particularly well. Read the label to be sure the fruit is canned in juice and not sugar-rich syrup. Ideally, you can buy fruit in glass jars or in cans manufactured without BPA, an unfriendly chemical you can read more about on page 80.

CHAPTER 8

Crunchy Extras

CRUNCHY SNACKS HAVE A REPUTATION for being pretty junky. The likes of nacho cheese–dusted chips and caramel-coated popcorn come to mind (both of which my kids have tried to slip quietly into the shopping cart). But it needn't always be so. Plenty of options are out there, store-bought and homemade, that are both tasty and wholesome—or at least not unhealthful.

Besides contributing nourishment, crunchy sides can also add interest to a main course. Consider, for example, how much more appealing a thermos of black beans is when accompanied by a stack of crispy baked tortilla chips. Similarly, a small handful of toasted pumpkin seeds can add texture and protein to a main-course salad.

Most of these snacks take longer to prepare than you are likely to have in the morning, so are best suited for after-school or weekend cooking. The DIY popcorn is the exception since it takes no time at all. Every one of them can be packed into lunch containers ahead of time, and if stored properly, most will stay good and crunchy for a week or so. And all weigh in at 50 to 120 calories a serving. For when you need the convenience of store-bought nibbles, you'll find suggestions for those in this chapter as well.

COCONUT
Granola Bark

MY GRANOLA IS A TEENY BIT FAMOUS—at least in my small circle of mom friends. The jar I donate to the school auction each spring always fetches a ridiculous sum. This granola bark is a twist on the original in which the oats are pressed firmly into a baking pan like a giant granola bar. Once it's cooked and cooled, break it into chunks, reserving any crumbs left behind for topping yogurt or fruit salad. If you want to turn this into a more traditional granola, spread the mixture loosely over two baking sheets instead of one, and bake until nicely browned.

MAKES ABOUT 48 PIECES; 1 OR 2 PIECES PER SERVING

3 cups rolled oats (not quick oats)

1 cup slivered almonds

1 cup unsweetened shredded coconut

¼ cup flax meal

¼ teaspoon salt

¼ cup pure maple syrup

½ cup firmly packed brown sugar

4 tablespoons water

¼ cup canola oil

1 egg white

1 teaspoon vanilla extract

1. Preheat the oven to 350°F. Line a 10-by-15-inch rimmed baking sheet with parchment paper so that it drapes a couple of inches over the two long sides.

2. In a medium bowl, mix together the oats, almonds, coconut, flax meal, and salt.

3. In a small saucepan, cook the maple syrup, brown sugar, and 1 table-spoon of the water over medium heat, stirring often, until the sugar dissolves, 1 to 2 minutes. Remove from the heat and set aside.

4. Add the remaining 3 tablespoons water, the canola oil, egg white, and vanilla to the oats mixture and stir until combined.

5. Drizzle the syrup mixture over the oats mixture and stir until combined.

6. Dump the granola onto the prepared baking sheet. With your hands, press the granola firmly and evenly onto the baking sheet, forming one giant rectangle of granola. (If it sticks to your hands, cover the granola with a piece of parchment paper as you work.)

7. Bake, turning halfway through baking, until the granola is golden brown in the center and darker brown around the edges, about 40 minutes.

8. Let cool on the baking sheet for 30 minutes. Using your hands, break the bark into pieces big enough for a couple of bites each. Stack in a roomy cookie tin for up to 1 week. Any remaining crumbly bits can be stored separately and used to top yogurt or cereal.

PUMPED-UP
Party Mix

MY RIFF ON CLASSIC PARTY MIX has all the savor and crunch of the original, it's just "pumped up" with healthful goodies: more whole-grain ingredients, nuts and seeds, and less butter. A dash of cayenne gives it a kick without being too spicy for little ones. Keep in mind that this is a very flexible recipe, so don't make yourself crazy tracking down exact ingredients. If you can't find whole-grain pretzels, just use regular ones. If your market sells only raw pumpkin seeds, use those and add an extra dash of salt. If you prefer cashews to peanuts, make the switch. It's tasty just out of the oven, but extra good the day after it's made.

MAKES 7 CUPS; ⅓ TO ½ CUP PER SERVING

3 cups whole-grain woven cereal, (or Rice or Corn Chex)

1½ cups salted whole-grain mini pretzels or pretzel sticks

1 cup salted whole-grain bagel chips, broken into bite-size pieces

¾ cup salted roasted peanuts or other favorite nuts

⅓ cup salted roasted pumpkin seeds (pepitas)

⅓ cup salted roasted sunflower seeds

2 tablespoons melted butter

3 tablespoons Worcestershire sauce

2 teaspoons Dijon mustard

2 teaspoons garlic powder

2 teaspoons paprika

2 dashes of cayenne pepper

¼ teaspoon salt

1. Preheat the oven to 300°F.

2. In a large bowl, mix together the cereal, pretzels, bagel chips, peanuts, pumpkin seeds, and sunflower seeds.

3. In a small bowl, whisk together the butter, Worcestershire sauce, mustard, garlic powder, paprika, cayenne, and salt until smooth. Drizzle over the cereal mixture and, using a rubber spatula, toss the ingredients together, until evenly coated with the butter mixture. It will take a number of turns with the spatula to do this thoroughly.

4. Spread the party mix evenly over two ungreased rimmed baking sheets.

5. Bake until the cereal is lightly browned, 20 to 25 minutes.

6. Let cool on the baking sheets for 30 minutes. Store in an airtight container for up to 1 week.

SKINNY MINI
Cheese Straws

THESE ARE A FAVORITE OF MY DAUGHTER VIRGINIA, who loves to help roll out the dough (and eat the finished product!). The combination of crunch and cheesiness makes them kind of addictive. Luckily, they're made with whole-wheat flour and wholesome ingredients, which means they're an improvement over most store-bought cheese crackers. I make them about half the length of typical cheese straws so they can easily fit into a lunch container.

MAKES ABOUT 80 MINI CHEESE STRAWS; 6 TO 8 STRAWS PER SERVING

---

1 cup whole-wheat pastry flour, plus more for rolling out the dough

4 tablespoons cold unsalted butter, cut into small cubes

1½ cups coarsely grated sharp Cheddar cheese

¼ cup finely grated Parmesan cheese

½ teaspoon salt

¼ cup milk

1. Preheat the oven to 350°F.

2. Put the flour in the bowl of a food processor fitted with a metal blade. Scatter the butter over the flour, and add the Cheddar, Parmesan, and salt. Process until the ingredients turn into a coarse meal, 10 to 15 seconds.

3. Drizzle the milk over the flour mixture while pulsing the food processor 10 to 15 times, until the dough forms moist clumps.

4. Turn the dough out onto a lightly floured work surface and pat together. Using a rolling pin, roll the dough into a 9-by-14-inch rectangle that is about ⅛ inch thick.

5. Using a large, sharp knife, cut the dough in half lengthwise. Then cut the dough crosswise into ⅓-inch-by-4½-inch strips. Place the cheese straws about ¼ inch apart on two ungreased baking sheets.

6. Bake until the cheese straws begin to darken around the edges and are light brown on top, 12 to 13 minutes.

7. Let cool on the baking sheets for 30 minutes. Store in an airtight container for up to 1 week.

NOTE: If you don't have a food processor, you can make the dough by hand. In a large bowl, add the flour and butter, tossing to coat the butter cubes with flour. Then, using a pastry cutter or fork, work the butter into the flour until it is the size of small peas and the dough is uniformly crumbly. You can also do this by pinching the butter and flour between your fingers. Next, add the Cheddar, Parmesan, and salt, and mix well with a fork. Pour the milk over the dough and gently knead it with your hands until it's an even consistency. Cut and bake as directed.

CINNAMON
Wonton Crisps

THE SAME THIN DOUGH THAT MAKES FRIED EGG ROLLS so light and crispy also works well for delicate baked crackers. Just brush wonton wrappers lightly with egg, sprinkle them with cinnamon-sugar, and toast them in the oven. Cutting the wontons on the diagonal is the quickest technique, or you can get creative and use cookie cutters to create charming shapes. For a variation, mix together 2 tablespoons sugar with 1½ tablespoons finely chopped fennel seed to use in place of the cinnamon-sugar.

MAKES 48 CRISPS; 6 TO 8 CRISPS PER SERVING

2 tablespoons sugar

1 teaspoon ground cinnamon

24 square wonton wrappers (see Note)

1 egg

1. Preheat the oven to 375°F.

2. In a small bowl, mix together the sugar and cinnamon.

3. Arrange the wonton wrappers in two stacks on your work surface and cut them in half on the diagonal. Place the wontons on two ungreased baking sheets, being sure that they don't overlap.

4. In another small bowl, whisk the egg with a fork. Using a pastry brush, lightly coat the top of the wonton wrappers on one of the baking sheets (work with just one pan at a time so the egg doesn't dry out before you add the cinnamon-sugar).

5. Sprinkle each egg-brushed wonton with a generous pinch or two of cinnamon-sugar.

6. Repeat with the second sheet of wontons.

7. Bake until the edges of the wontons turn golden brown, 5 to 6 minutes.

8. Let cool on the baking sheets for 20 minutes. Store in an airtight container for up to 5 days.

NOTE: Wonton wrappers are sold in the produce or refrigerated section (near the tofu) of many supermarkets, organic markets, and Asian markets. You can freeze wrappers you don't use.

"BETCHA CAN'T EAT JUST ONE"

Parmesan Kale Chips

WE WERE GETTING SO MUCH KALE in our weekly produce box, it felt like a part-time job just to keep up with it. My kids were ready to stage a boycott. Then I started experimenting with kale chips and found them surprisingly tasty. Four out of the five people in our household are fans, which is pretty good odds considering it's kale we're talking about. This recipe might strike you as a little strange—cashew butter and Parmesan cheese?—but the result is a tangy, cheesy chip that holds its crunch.

MAKES ABOUT 8 SNACK-SIZE SERVINGS

1 medium bunch flat or curly leaf kale (about 8 ounces)

¼ cup salted roasted cashew butter

2 tablespoons fresh lemon juice

⅓ cup warm water

¼ cup finely grated Parmesan cheese

1. Preheat the oven to 275°F.

2. Remove the stems from the kale, and reserve for another use or discard. Tear the leaves into pieces that are about the size of potato chips. Wash and dry thoroughly. (A salad spinner works well for this.) You should have four generous handfuls of kale.

3. In a large bowl, add the cashew butter, lemon juice, and warm water. With a fork, mix together until creamy and smooth. It might seem as though the ingredients won't come together but, with a little elbow grease, they will in a minute or two.

4. Add the kale pieces to the bowl and, using a rubber spatula, stir until they're coated with the cashew butter mixture. Kale is hearty, so don't be timid about pressing down until it is evenly coated and no liquid remains in the bottom of the bowl. Use your hands if that helps.

5. Place the kale pieces on two ungreased baking sheets, all bunched together. Sprinkle the cheese over the top of the kale, ensuring every piece gets showered with cheese.

6. Spread out the kale pieces on the baking sheets. It's OK if the pieces are touching, but not overlapping.

7. Bake until the cheese is golden brown and the chips are crisp, about 45 minutes. Chips that are still a little soft in the center need to continue baking until crispy.

8. Let cool on the baking sheets for 20 minutes. Store in an airtight container for up to 5 days.

DIY
Microwave Popcorn

BELIEVE IT OR NOT, you can cook your own microwave popcorn using a brown paper lunch bag. When we discovered this trick in our house, it became a near daily ritual for my daughter Isabelle, who loves popcorn as a lunch-box snack. You can get creative by adding a couple of dashes of cinnamon, chili powder, or other favorite spice, or a sprinkling of Parmesan cheese. Don't be freaked out by the staples on the paper bag. They're too tiny to cause a reaction in your microwave.

MAKES ABOUT 5 CUPS; 5 SERVINGS

¼ cup popcorn kernels

1 tablespoon melted butter

Generous pinch of salt

Special equipment

1 brown paper lunch bag

Stapler

1. Pour the popcorn kernels into the brown paper bag. Seal the bag by folding it over ½ inch at the top, twice, pressing down firmly. Fasten the bag together with two staples.

2. Lay the bag horizontally on a microwave-safe plate in the microwave. Cook on high until the popping becomes irregular, 2½ to 3 minutes.

3. Remove the bag carefully from the microwave—it will be hot. Open the bag and discard the staples.

4. Drizzle the butter over the popcorn, add the salt, close the bag, and give it a good shake until the popcorn is evenly coated with butter and salt. Taste and add more salt if needed.

5. Store in an airtight container for up to 2 days.

NOTE: You can make this popcorn without stapling the bag. Be sure to fold the bag as tightly as possible and be aware that the kernels may not pop as well as when the bag is stapled.

Crunchy Choices

Landing on snacks that meet your approval from a health standpoint isn't easy. The superprocessed options far outweigh the wholesome ones. But it's not hopeless, as new, more nourishing snacks seem to be showing up on supermarket shelves all the time.

Here are some of the better crunchy choices in the snack department. Be sure to read the labels since some brands are more healthful than others:

seasoned roasted seaweed

freeze-dried vegetables

crispy snap peas

crispy baked apple chips

soy nuts

roasted peanuts

salted roasted pistachios

tamari roasted almonds

salted roasted sunflower seeds and pumpkin seeds

kale chips

pretzels and pretzel thins, especially whole-grain

popcorn made with natural ingredients

low-sugar whole-grain cereal

baked lentil chips

whole-grain pita chips

baked corn tortilla chips

graham crackers, especially whole-wheat

lightly salted mini rice cakes made with brown rice

soy rice crisps made with natural ingredients

Asian brown rice crackers

HOMESPUN HUNDRED-CALORIE BAGS

Knock off food marketers' "100-calorie bag" idea by prepackaging your own single-serving snacks. It allows you to be choosy about the snacks you buy, save money, and be more eco-friendly (if you use wax-paper bags or reusable containers).

CHAPTER 9

Goodies

AS A NUTRITION PROFESSIONAL, I know that we're supposed to love our children with reassuring words and generous hugs—and not with sweets. But there's something eminently, well, sweet, about nestling a little crock of pudding or a homemade chocolate chip cookie into their lunch boxes to be discovered later that day. When meals are chock-full of nutritious, low-fat, wholesome foods, there is indeed some wiggle room for goodies.

The key to lunch-box confections is to aim for quality ingredients, keep portions moderate, and consider them a "sometimes" treat instead of an "everyday" food. Luckily, these recipes are lighter in sugar and richer in whole grains, nuts, seeds, and even vegetables than typical sweets. Several of them make a generous batch, which means you'll have plenty on hand for lunches, to send into school for class celebrations, or, in some cases, to store in the freezer for another day.

Make these goodies with your kids and pour loads of love into every stir. That's the best ingredient for delicious desserts.

COCOA-DUSTED
Almonds

I CAME UP WITH THIS RECIPE after learning that the store-bought cocoa almonds I love are made with artificial flavors and not one, but two, artificial sweeteners. This homemade version, with just a handful of ingredients, takes less than 5 minutes to knock out and is a favorite lunchtime pick-me-up. As far as nuts go, almonds are particularly rich in protein, fiber, and vitamin E. I usually pack my kids about ten of these in a tiny container; just enough to tickle their sweet tooth.

MAKES 2 CUPS; 10 TO 12 ALMONDS PER SERVING

2 cups raw almonds (not roasted or salted)

1 tablespoon canola oil

⅓ cup sweetened cocoa powder (see Note)

1 teaspoon unsweetened cocoa powder

2 pinches of salt

1. Preheat the oven to 300°F. Line two baking sheets with parchment paper.

2. In a large, shallow bowl, add the almonds and drizzle with the canola oil. Using your hands, toss the almonds until evenly coated. Sprinkle the sweetened cocoa powder, unsweetened cocoa powder, and salt over the almonds. Using a rubber spatula, turn the almonds into the cocoa powder until they are evenly coated. It takes ten or more turns to adequately dust the almonds with cocoa.

3. Transfer the almonds to the prepared baking sheets, and bake until toasted, 15 to 20 minutes. When the almonds are fragrant, they're done.

4. Let cool on the baking sheet for 20 minutes. Store in an airtight container for up to 2 weeks.

NOTE: Do not use hot cocoa mix, which is made with dry milk powder. Sweetened cocoa powder is essentially just cocoa and sugar.

ROSIE'S
Energy Balls

THESE CHEWY TREATS are a variation on the first recipe my daughter Rosie ever brought home. She proudly marched in with a batch of them from preschool and presented me with the instructions. They're sweet and filling with a texture that makes them seem a little like candy. With a full cup of dried milk powder, they also supply a decent dose of calcium. On rushed mornings, my kids have been known to grab a couple for on-the-go breakfasts.

MAKES ABOUT 20 BALLS; 1 OR 2 BALLS PER SERVING

½ cup natural unsweetened creamy peanut butter or other nut, soy nut, or seed butter

½ cup honey

1 cup instant nonfat dry milk powder

¼ cup flax meal

1. In a medium bowl, stir together the peanut butter, honey, milk powder, and flax meal with a wooden spoon. Once you've gotten things partially mixed, work the batter with your hands until a smooth dough forms.

2. With your hands, break off pieces of dough and roll into 1¼-inch balls. Arrange in a container big enough to accommodate them in a single layer.

3. Refrigerate for at least 30 minutes before eating. Store in an airtight container for up to 1 week in the refrigerator or up to 3 weeks in the freezer.

SOUR CHERRY
Oatmeal Bars

THE SWEET-TART TASTE OF SOUR CHERRY JAM over a crumbly, brown sugar–sweetened dough is pretty scrumptious. The recipe is a twist on a fruit crisp I've been making for years, only in this version the crust shows up on both top and bottom, and jam subs in for fresh fruit. I cut the bars into petite squares that are just big enough for a lunch-box treat (or an after-school snack along with a glass of cold milk). If you can't get your hands on a jar of sour cherry jam, feel free to substitute apricot or raspberry instead.

MAKES 20 BARS

1 cup whole-wheat pastry flour

½ cup rolled oats (not quick oats)

½ cup firmly packed brown sugar

½ teaspoon baking powder

¼ teaspoon salt

6 tablespoons unsalted butter, at room temperature

½ cup finely chopped walnuts

¾ cup sour cherry jam

1. Preheat the oven to 350°F. Line an 8-inch square baking pan with parchment paper so that it drapes a couple of inches over two sides.

2. In a large bowl, add the flour, oats, brown sugar, baking powder, and salt and stir with a fork. Add the butter and, using an electric mixer on low speed, mix until the ingredients form a uniformly crumbly mixture, about 45 seconds. Add the walnuts and continue mixing on low speed until they are evenly distributed, about 5 seconds.

3. With your hands, press two-thirds of the dough firmly and evenly into the bottom of the prepared baking pan. (If the dough sticks to your hands, cover it with a piece of parchment paper as you work.)

4. With a spoon, spread the jam evenly over the dough. Sprinkle the remaining one-third of the dough evenly over the jam. You will see the jam peeking through.

5. Bake until the top is deep brown and the jam along the edges begins to darken, 45 to 50 minutes.

6. Let cool in the baking pan for 30 minutes.

7. Run a knife along the two sides of the pan that don't have an overhang of parchment paper. Grab the two ends of parchment paper and carefully lift out the sour cherry oatmeal square and transfer to a cutting board.

8. Cut into 20 bars. Store in an airtight container for up to 5 days in the pantry or 2 weeks in the freezer.

CHOCOLATE CHIP–
Pretzel
Cookies

WHEN IT COMES TO BAKING, chocolate chip cookies are the number-one pick, by far, among all three of my kids. They like this recipe because it's got enough chocolate to feel like a treat, plus they get to dump pretzels into the mix. I like it because it's made with two different whole grains and is more moderate in the butter and sugar department than a lot of cookies. You can leave the nuts out entirely if your crew doesn't like them, or sub in raisins or dried cranberries.

MAKES ABOUT 36 COOKIES; 1 OR 2 COOKIES PER SERVING

¾ cup whole-wheat pastry flour

¾ cup rolled oats (not quick oats)

½ teaspoon baking soda

6 tablespoons unsalted butter, at room temperature

¼ cup granulated sugar

½ cup firmly packed brown sugar

½ teaspoon vanilla extract

1 egg

⅔ cup bittersweet or semisweet chocolate chips

½ cup salted roasted shelled pistachios

1½ cups salted mini pretzels (preferably whole-grain pretzels)

1. Preheat the oven to 350°F. Line three baking sheets with parchment paper.

2. In a medium bowl, add the flour, oats, and baking soda and stir with a fork.

3. Using an electric mixer on medium speed, in a large bowl, beat together the butter, granulated sugar, and brown sugar until creamy, 1 to 2 minutes. Add the vanilla and egg, and beat again until smooth, about 30 seconds.

4. With the mixer on low speed, add the flour-oats mixture to the sugar mixture, a little at a time, scraping down the sides as needed, until smooth.

5. Add the chocolate chips and pistachios to the dough, and continue beating on low speed until just combined. Add the pretzels and beat for another 10 seconds to break them up a little and incorporate them into the dough.

6. Drop rounded tablespoonfuls of dough about 2 inches apart on the prepared baking sheets.

7. Bake until the cookies are golden brown around the edges, 10 to 12 minutes.

8. Let cool on the baking sheets for a few minutes, then transfer to a wire rack to cool completely. Store in an airtight container for up to 5 days in the pantry or up to 2 weeks in the freezer.

PETITE PUMPKIN
Gingerbread
Cupcakes

WHAT COULD FEEL MORE LIKE A TREAT than miniature cupcakes? This is just the sort of goody to bring to school for birthdays and other celebrations. The cakes themselves are quite wholesome; the frosting is undeniably decadent. Even so, each miniature treat weighs in at only about 100 calories.

MAKES 36 MINI CUPCAKES

---

2 cups whole-wheat pastry flour

1 teaspoon baking soda

1 teaspoon baking powder

¼ teaspoon salt

1 teaspoon ground cinnamon

2 teaspoons ground ginger

½ teaspoon ground cloves

⅓ cup canola oil

⅔ cup firmly packed brown sugar

⅓ cup pure maple syrup

1 egg

1 teaspoon vanilla extract

¾ cup canned pumpkin purée (not pumpkin pie filling)

⅔ cup low-fat buttermilk (see No Buttermilk? No Problem, page 128)

Cream Cheese Frosting

4 ounces Neufchâtel cheese, at room temperature (see Note)

4 tablespoons unsalted butter, at room temperature

1¼ cups confectioners' sugar

2 tablespoons pure maple syrup

Special equipment

Cupcake tins for 36 mini cupcakes (see Note)

(continued)

NOTE: If you don't have mini-cupcake tins, this recipe will make a dozen standard-size cupcakes and will take an additional 8 to 10 minutes to bake. Cut them in half for a lunch box–size portion.

Neufchâtel is naturally about 30 percent lower in fat than cream cheese but with a similar taste and texture. Substitute regular cream cheese if you can't find Neufchâtel.

1. Preheat the oven to 350°F. Grease the mini cupcake tins with oil or line with cupcake paper liners.

2. In a medium bowl, whisk together the flour, baking soda, baking powder, salt, cinnamon, ginger, and cloves.

3. Using an electric mixer on medium speed, in a large bowl, beat together the canola oil, brown sugar, maple syrup, egg, vanilla, and pumpkin purée until smooth, scraping down the sides as needed, about 2 minutes.

4. Reduce the speed to medium-low. Add the flour mixture to the pumpkin mixture in three additions, alternating with the buttermilk in two additions, scraping down the sides after each addition, beating until the batter is creamy and smooth, another minute or so.

5. Divide the batter among the cupcake tins, filling them nearly to the top. Bake until a toothpick inserted in the center of a cupcake comes out clean, 13 to 14 minutes.

6. Let cool completely in the cupcake tins.

7. Meanwhile, to make the frosting: In a medium bowl, add the Neufchâtel cheese, butter, confectioners' sugar, and maple syrup and stir vigorously with a fork until creamy.

8. Spread the frosting on the cooled cupcakes.

9. Cover the cupcakes in plastic wrap. Store in the refrigerator for up to 2 days. Unfrosted cupcakes can be stored in the freezer for up to 1 month.

NO BUTTERMILK? NO PROBLEM

If you don't want to make a special trip to the market for buttermilk, here is a little trick I use for baking. For every 1 cup of buttermilk needed, measure out 1 cup minus 1 tablespoon of milk. Add 1 tablespoon lemon juice or white wine vinegar. Let it sit on the counter for 5 minutes to thicken. Then proceed according to your recipe.

If you do buy buttermilk, you can always freeze what you don't use.

TENDER CRANBERRY
Streusel Muffins

CRANBERRY MUFFINS WERE A WINTER STAPLE in my house growing up, always with cinnamon-sugar sprinkled on top. Cranberries are a cold-weather fruit that add tang, color, and loads of antioxidants to this muffin. Fresh cranberries are ideal, but thawed frozen ones yield good results as well. You can also use unpeeled chopped apples or whole fresh blueberries instead, depending on the season.

MAKES 48 MINI MUFFINS OR 14 STANDARD-SIZE MUFFINS

2⅓ cups fresh or thawed frozen cranberries

1 cup whole-wheat pastry flour

1 cup oat flour (see Note)

2 tablespoons flax meal

1 teaspoon baking powder

½ teaspoon baking soda

½ teaspoon salt

¾ cup low-fat buttermilk (see No Buttermilk? No Problem, page 128)

1 egg

⅓ cup fresh orange juice

Zest from ½ large orange

¾ cup granulated sugar

3 tablespoons melted butter

Streusel Topping

2 tablespoons rolled oats (not quick oats)

2 tablespoons firmly packed brown sugar

½ teaspoon ground cinnamon

Special equipment

Muffin tins for 48 mini muffins or 14 standard muffins

NOTE: If you don't have oat flour in your pantry, you can make it by pulverizing rolled oats in the bowl of a food processor fitted with a metal blade until it becomes the fine-grain texture of flour.

1. Preheat the oven to 375°F. Grease the muffin tins with oil or line with paper liners.

2. Coarsely chop the cranberries with a knife or by pulsing them a few times in a food processor fitted with a metal blade. Set aside.

3. In a medium bowl, whisk together the whole-wheat pastry flour, oat flour, flax meal, baking powder, baking soda, and salt.

4. In another medium bowl, whisk together the buttermilk, egg, orange juice, orange zest, and granulated sugar until smooth. Slowly drizzle in the melted butter, whisking constantly, until combined.

5. Add the buttermilk mixture to the flour mixture, using a rubber spatula to gently stir them together until just combined. Add the cranberries, stirring with as few strokes as possible. If you stir the batter too much, it will result in tougher muffins (we want tough kids, not tough muffins!).

6. Divide the batter among the muffin tins, filling them about three-quarters full.

7. To make the streusel topping: In a small bowl, add the oats, brown sugar, and cinnamon and stir with a fork. Sprinkle the topping over the batter, dividing it evenly.

8. Bake until a toothpick inserted into the center of a muffin comes out clean, 12 to 15 minutes for mini muffins, 20 to 25 minutes for standard-size muffins.

9. Let cool in the muffin tins for 30 minutes. Store in an airtight container for up to 3 days in the pantry or up to 1 month in the freezer.

EVERYBODY LOVES
Chocolate Pudding

NOTHING IS HOMIER than a little crock of chocolate pudding in a lunch box. This one, made with milk, antioxidant-rich chocolate, and an egg for added richness, manages to pack in some nutrition with every decadent-tasting bite. It's so good, you'll want to be sure to leave a little in the fridge for yourself before packing it off to school.

MAKES ABOUT 2 ⅓ CUPS; 5 SERVINGS

---

1 egg

3 tablespoons cornstarch

¼ cup light agave nectar

2 tablespoons unsweetened cocoa powder

1 teaspoon vanilla extract

Pinch of salt

2 cups milk, preferably 1 percent

1½ ounces finely chopped bittersweet chocolate

1. In a small bowl, whisk together the egg, cornstarch, agave nectar, cocoa powder, vanilla, and salt.

2. In a medium saucepan, heat the milk over medium heat. When tiny bubbles appear all around the edge of the pan, add the chocolate, whisking constantly, until melted and smooth, about 1 minute. Remove from the heat.

3. Scoop up about ⅓ cup of the heated chocolate milk and slowly drizzle it into the egg mixture, whisking constantly, until smooth, about 30 seconds. Then slowly drizzle the egg-chocolate milk mixture back into the saucepan, whisking constantly, about 30 seconds. Be careful not to combine the hot liquid with the raw egg too quickly, or it may result in scrambled chocolate eggs, not chocolate pudding!

4. Return the saucepan to medium-high heat and cook for 1 to 2 minutes, stirring constantly with a wooden spoon, until the pudding thickens enough that a defined line remains when you run the spoon through the center.

5. Transfer the pudding to a medium bowl, cover, and refrigerate until chilled, about 2 hours. If desired, lay a piece of plastic wrap directly on the surface of the pudding to prevent a skin from forming on the top.

6. Pack into small containers and store in the refrigerator for up to 3 days.

Eight Lunch-Box Loving Touches

There are loads of ways to fill a lunch box with tenderness beyond sweet things to eat. Here are a few fresh and fun ideas to add to the time-tested lunch-box love note:

1. Use an indelible pen to draw a face on a tangerine.

2. Include a couple of stickers.

3. Write your child a note on a banana.

4. Jot down a riddle or joke he or she can share with friends.

5. Include a silly little poem.

6. Write a couple of math problems.

7. Sketch one half of a picture, leaving the second half for your child to finish.

8. Include a card for birthdays, holidays, and special celebrations.

Ten Petite Treats

Here are quick and easy goodies that take little time to prepare but are sure to elicit a smile:

1. Small square of good-quality chocolate

2. Fortune cookie

3. Graham cracker sandwiching melted chocolate chips

4. Dehydrated strawberries, apples, or pineapple

5. Fig bar

6. Honey stick

7. Small container of all-natural pudding

8. Mixture of chocolate chips and dried cranberries

9. Strawberries and a small container of whipped cream for dipping

10. All-natural animal crackers

After School

No matter how well-proportioned, balanced, and jam-packed the lunch boxes might be when I put them into my kids' hands each morning, at least one of my girls comes home ravenous at the end of the day. And while it's tempting to toss them a bag of chips and move on, that's not likely to sustain them for long. The trick is to nourish kids enough so they'll last through the after-noon, but not so heartily that they want to take a pass at dinnertime. The best afternoon snacks are the ones that hit some of the same nutritional high notes you aim for at lunch: grains, protein foods, healthful fats, fruits, and vegetables, all delivered without a lot of processed ingredients. Kids need quality snacks to fuel their brains and bodies as they tackle homework, music lessons, sports, and whatever else happens between school and supper.

CHAPTER 10

Tide-Me-Overs

HANDING YOUR CHILD A SNACK is often the first interaction you have with them after they've been at school all day. You want them to love it, and you want to feel good about what you feed them. These scrumptious snacks do both. Since after-school noshing often takes place heading from one activity to the next, portability is key. It's also nice to have options that can be made ahead of time rather than pulled together at the last minute. Look for the "make ahead notes" at the bottom of each recipe, which spells out which ones work on the go and which can be assembled in advance.

"PERFECT EVERY TIME"
Hard-Boiled Eggs

HARD-BOILED EGGS are the perfect food: portable, nutritious, and filling. One egg packs in high-quality protein, iron, and a number of other nutrients, at only 70 calories a pop. This technique for boiling them is pretty simple and prevents the yolk from developing the green rim that some kids find off-putting. I like to cook several at once for breakfasts, lunches, and snacks.

MAKES 4 SERVINGS

4 eggs

1. Have ready a large bowl of ice water.

2. Put eggs in a pot large enough to accommodate them and cover by 1 inch with water. Set over high heat and bring to a rolling boil. Cover the pot and remove from the heat. Wait for 12 minutes.

3. Using a slotted spoon, transfer eggs to the ice water to cool for 1 minute or so. Store in a container in the refrigerator for up to 1 week.

MAKE AHEAD NOTES: highly portable; a good make-ahead option.

TIP: SO SIMPLE DEVILED EGGS

For a speedy, deviled egg, start with a peeled hard-boiled egg. Cut in half lengthwise, scoop out the cooked yolk, and put into a small bowl. Add 2 teaspoons of mayonnaise, a pinch of salt, and a couple grinds of pepper. Mash with a fork until creamy. Fill the hollow of each egg half with the yolk mixture. Top with a dash of paprika or a pinch of fresh minced chives. To pack on the go, sandwich the two deviled egg halves together and store in a snug container.

THE COMFORT OF

Cottage Cheese and Crackers

POOR COTTAGE CHEESE . . . if you can look past its humble curds, you'll find something both nourishing and satisfying. This recipe was my grandmother's, and my mother always made it when we had company. My kids gobble it down, just as I did, using crackers and crunchy vegetables to do the scooping.

MAKES 2 OR 3 SERVINGS

1 cup low-fat cottage cheese

1 tablespoon mayonnaise

1½ tablespoons minced fresh parsley

2 tablespoons finely chopped red onion

Freshly ground pepper

Whole-grain crackers and/or sliced bell peppers, celery, or carrots

1 In a small bowl, add the cottage cheese, mayonnaise, parsley, onion, and a few generous grinds of pepper and stir until combined.

2 Serve with crackers and/or vegetables.

MAKE AHEAD NOTES: portable; a good make-ahead option. For an on-the-go snack, pack the cottage cheese in one container and the crackers or veggies in another.

ITALIAN
Quesadilla

THIS RECIPE takes what has to be one of the all time kid-favorites—quesadillas—and adds a flavorful spin with Italian cheeses, fresh basil, and sun-dried tomatoes. It calls for sliced rather than grated cheese since that's how provolone is often sold. While best hot out of the pan, it's still tasty at room temp for kids on the run. Be sure to cook the tortillas until they are good and crispy, and let the quesadilla cool for a minute or so before digging in so the hot and bubbly cheese doesn't burn little mouths.

MAKES 2 SERVINGS

2 thin slices provolone cheese

Two 8-inch whole-wheat flour tortillas

2 tablespoons finely grated Parmesan cheese

4 large oil-packed sun-dried tomatoes, chopped

4 medium fresh basil leaves, each torn into 3 or 4 pieces

⅓ cup loosely packed baby spinach

1 teaspoon extra-virgin olive oil

1. Tear one slice of provolone into eight pieces and lay them evenly over one tortilla. Sprinkle the Parmesan cheese over the provolone. Scatter the sun-dried tomatoes over the cheeses, followed by the basil leaves and the spinach. Tear the remaining slice of provolone into eight pieces and lay them over everything else. Top with the remaining tortilla.

2. In a medium skillet, heat the olive oil over medium-high heat. Put the quesadilla in the pan and cook until golden brown and crispy, 2 to 3 minutes. With a wide spatula, carefully flip the quesadilla and cook until the second side is browned, about 2 minutes.

3. Transfer the quesadilla to a cutting board and let cool for a few minutes. Cut into six wedges.

MAKE AHEAD NOTES: portable; can be made ahead, but best hot out of the pan.

CRISPY
Applewiches

SMEAR PEANUT BUTTER or your favorite nut or seed butter between juicy slabs of apple, and you've got a crunchy, satisfying alternative to a traditional sandwich. Granola adds texture and a bit more heft to hold the kids' appetite until dinner. This recipe works beautifully as a lunch-box main as well.

MAKES 1 OR 2 SERVINGS

1 large apple

½ lemon

2 tablespoons peanut, tree nut, or seed butter

2 tablespoons granola

1 Use an apple corer or melon baller to remove the apple's core.

2 Cut ½ inch off of the top and bottom of the apple (nibble those while you work or discard). Cut the apple crosswise into four ½-inch-thick slices. They will look like bagels with holes in the center.

3 Rub the cut side of the lemon over both sides of the apple slices to keep them from browning.

4 Spread the peanut butter on two of the apple slices. Sprinkle the granola over the peanut butter. Top with the remaining apple slices.

MAKE AHEAD NOTES: highly portable; a good make-ahead option.

OUT-OF-THE-BOX

Peanut Butter Granola Bars

BAKING IS ONE OF THE BEST WAYS to get kids into the kitchen. While my three girls love to make cookies, I'm always on the lookout for something a little more wholesome that's still appealing. This fills the bill on both counts. My kids love coming home to a plate of these lip-smackers. I serve them still warm from the oven along with glasses of cold milk.

MAKES 18 BARS

1 cup rolled oats (not quick oats)

⅔ cup crispy brown rice cereal or Rice Krispies

⅓ cup flax meal

⅓ cup bittersweet or semisweet chocolate chips

⅓ cup dried cherries or dried cranberries

¼ cup organic brown rice syrup (see Note)

1 tablespoon pure maple syrup

1 tablespoon canola oil

1 tablespoon water

¼ cup natural unsweetened creamy peanut butter or other nut or seed butter

1. Preheat the oven to 350°F. Line an 8-inch square baking pan with parchment paper so that it drapes a couple of inches over two sides.

2. In a medium bowl, mix together the oats, cereal, flax meal, chocolate chips, and dried cherries.

3. In a small bowl, stir together the brown rice syrup, maple syrup, canola oil, water, and peanut butter until smooth.

4. Drizzle the syrup mixture over the oats mixture and stir until combined. The batter will be thick, sticky, and a little stubborn.

5. Dump the mixture into the prepared baking pan. With your hands, press the mixture firmly and evenly into the bottom of the prepared baking pan. (If the mixture sticks to your hands, cover it with a piece of parchment paper as you work.)

6. Bake until the granola is golden brown on the top and darker brown around the edges, 30 to 35 minutes.

7. Let cool in the pan for 30 minutes. Cut into 18 bars.

8. Store in an airtight container for up to 5 days in the pantry or 2 weeks in the freezer.

MAKE AHEAD NOTES: highly portable; a good make-ahead option.

NOTE: If you don't have brown rice syrup, substitute honey. The bars will be more crumbly but still tasty.

Raising the Bar on Granola

I have conflicted feelings about packaged granola bars: I love the convenience, but I don't always like the ingredients or the excessive packaging. The fact that manufacturers add a boatload of "vitamins and minerals" doesn't offset the sugar, artificial flavors, colors, and preservatives that are sometimes in there, too. If I'm going to give my kids a sweet, I'll give them a sweet. I'd rather it not masquerade as health food. Here are some guidelines to help you buy a better bar.

Less sugar: Aim for about 8 grams of sugar or less per bar. Keep in mind that dried fruits naturally contain sugar, so allow a little wiggle room for bars with raisins, dried cherries, and the like.

More fiber: At least 2 grams of fiber per serving is a good goal, and more is even better. Look for the words "whole grains" among the ingredients, which pack in more fiber and nutrients than processed ones.

Fewer calories: Some bars top 200 calories, which is a lot, especially for littler appetites, and particularly if you are pairing the snack with a glass of milk. Opt for bars that are less than 150 calories.

Familiar foods: Read the label and look for wholesome ingredients. Skip any bars that include partially hydrogenated fats, or any other ingredient a typical school kid couldn't identify.

Eight After-School Eats

Here are eight easy-to-make healthful snacks to hold your kids over until dinner is on the table.

1. **Speedy Parfait:** Layer low-fat yogurt, fruit, granola, and a drizzle of honey or maple syrup for a quick parfait.

2. **Tortilla Roll-Up:** Put shredded lettuce, grated carrot, grated cheese, and a few dashes of taco sauce on a whole-wheat flour tortilla and roll up.

3. **Chocolate Grahamwich:** Break a graham cracker in half. In a toaster oven, melt chocolate chips on one half and spread with a knife. Smear the other half with your favorite nut or seed butter. Press the two halves together to make a sandwich.

4. **Hot Cereal:** Make a batch of hot cereal such as oatmeal or wheat farina with low-fat milk. Top with fresh or dried fruit.

5. **Notch-Above Nachos:** To make nachos that are more nourishing than most, layer baked tortilla chips, plenty of black beans, a sprinkling of cheese, and salsa. Melt it all in the toaster oven.

6. **Soup's On:** Heat up homemade or store-bought soup. Chicken noodle, tomato, and minestrone are kid favorites. Toss in some extra veggies for good measure.

7. **Pancake Sandwich:** Spread leftover pancakes or whole-grain toaster waffles with low-fat Greek yogurt or cream cheese, fresh fruit, and a little maple syrup.

8. **Lettuce Wrap:** Wrap a big crunchy lettuce leaf, a slice of turkey, matchstick slices of crunchy veggies, and a dab of mustard around a mozzarella cheese stick.

DREAMY
Mango-Orange Pops

CALL ME CRAZY, but I've been known to give these nourishing pops to my kids for breakfast. There are two whole oranges in the recipe, something you're not likely to find in store-bought brands. The yogurt lends a protein boost that will help fill up kids' tummies longer than standard juice pops. If you can't wait for the pops to freeze, enjoy them as frothy drinks over ice.

MAKES 10 POPS

2 medium seedless Valencia oranges

1 cup unsweetened mango juice (see Note)

1½ cups nonfat vanilla yogurt

1 teaspoon vanilla extract

Special equipment

Ten 3-ounce popsicle molds

1. Set the oranges on a cutting board. Using a serrated knife, cut off the peel and pith of each orange, following the curve of the fruit. Cut each orange into quarters.

2. Pour the mango juice into a blender, followed by the oranges, yogurt, and vanilla. Blend until creamy and smooth with no chunks of fruit remaining, about 1 minute.

3. Pour into ten molds and freeze for at least 6 hours.

MAKE AHEAD NOTES: portable if pulled from the freezer and wrapped in parchment paper just before picking up from school; a good make-ahead option.

NOTE: You can substitute orange or mango-orange juice along with 1 tablespoon honey for the mango juice.

CREAMY
Banana Shake

EVEN IF BANANA SHAKES aren't your "thing," don't overlook this one. The first time I made it, I found myself downing the whole contents of the blender myself; not a drop was left for the kids. Although it doesn't have a smidgen of ice cream, it qualifies as a shake since it has all the requisite frothy deliciousness. As an option, you can add 1 tablespoon of peanut butter and 2 teaspoons of unsweetened cocoa powder to make it even more luscious. Be sure to freeze the banana first, since that's the secret to the creamy texture.

MAKES 2 SERVINGS

1 cup milk, preferably 1 percent

1½ medium frozen ripe bananas, cut into 6 pieces

2 teaspoons honey

1 teaspoon vanilla extract

4 ice cubes

1. Pour the milk into a blender, followed by the banana, honey, vanilla, and ice. Blend until creamy and smooth with no banana chunks or ice chips remaining, about 1 minute.

2. Pour into two cups.

MAKE AHEAD NOTES: portable if made just before snack time and packed into to-go cups with straws.

A SMOOTHIE SECRET: FROZEN BANANAS

I rely on frozen bananas in nearly all of my smoothies. They're naturally sweet and create the same sort of creaminess you might expect from ice cream or frozen yogurt. Plus, smoothies are a great way to use up bananas in the fruit bowl when they start to go south. Wait until the bananas are good and ripe, peel, and then pop them into a resealable bag or container in the freezer. When making smoothies, cut frozen bananas into chunks or slices before adding to the blender.

Raspberry
SNEAK

WITH THE CREAMY TEXTURE, tangy flavor, and pink color of this smoothie, few would guess a full cup of spinach is in there, too. If you are worried your crew will be spinach-averse, start with ½ cup and then work your way up. Stock a supply of travel cups with straws to make on-the-go smoothies for your after-school crowd. The sweetness of vanilla yogurt can vary, so add more honey if needed.

MAKES 2 SERVINGS

¾ cup unsweetened apple juice

1 medium frozen ripe banana, cut into 4 pieces

1 cup frozen raspberries

1 cup unpacked baby spinach

One 6-ounce container nonfat vanilla yogurt (about ⅔ cup)

1 teaspoon vanilla extract

2 teaspoons honey, plus more if needed

1. Pour the apple juice into a blender, followed by the banana, raspberries, spinach, yogurt, vanilla, and honey. Blend until creamy and smooth with no chunks of fruit remaining, about 1 minute.

2. Pour into two cups.

MAKE AHEAD NOTES: portable if made just before snack time and packed into to-go cups with straws.

Mom-Approved Lunch-Box Supplies

Having a well-stocked "pantry" of lunch-packing supplies not only makes the job go more smoothly, it also cuts down enormously on all those little plastic baggies. Unfortunately, all reusable containers aren't created equal. Some have lead paint, contain phthalates, BPAs, and other chemicals you don't want near your child, much less his or her food. Here are a few pointers to keep a lid on toxins in your child's lunch box: Look for lightweight stainless-steel or plastic storage containers with the numbers 2, 4, or 5, which usually appear on the bottom. Avoid products marked with a 3, 6, or 7. Some experts also recommend avoiding plastic containers with the number 1. Glass containers are excellent for home use, but banging around in a kid's lunch? Probably not a good idea. As far as water bottles go, stainless steel is ideal. You can also look for BPA-free plastic and aluminum bottles.

LUNCH BOXES

Pottery Barn Kids: A one-stop resource for lunch-packing supplies, including a wide selection of charming lunch boxes. www.potterybarnkids.com

LL Bean: Good, basic, affordable lunch boxes in a variety of colors and designs. www.llbean.com

Oré: Insulated, laminated cotton-canvas lunch boxes shaped like a brown paper bag with colorful graphics. www.oreoriginals.com

BENTOS

Planet Box: Insulated lunch boxes with a compartmentalized stainless-steel insert for easy packing and cleanup. www.planetbox.com

ECOlunchbox: The sleek design of these stainless-steel stackables, along with the attractive carry bags, especially appeal to older kids. www.ecolunchboxes.com

STORAGE CONTAINERS

LunchBots: Stainless-steel containers in a rainbow of bright and charming colors. www.lunchbots.com

Rubbermaid: Affordable, BPA-free plastics, including Lunchblox, a line of containers that fit together like a set of blocks and include freezer packs. www.rubbermaid.com

HOT-FOOD CONTAINERS

Thermos: The classic container for keeping food warm during the school day, especially the sturdy 10-ounce food jar; also sells a variety of other lunch storage wares. www.thermos.com

Kids Konserve: Leakproof insulated food jars with colored lids; also makes sturdy stainless-steel containers. www.kidskonserve.com

WATER BOTTLES

Klean Kanteen: Durable stainless-steel water bottles available in a kid-friendly 12-ounce size. www.kleankanteen.com

Camelbak: BPA-free plastic bottles with a built-in straw makes lunchtime hydrating easy. www.camelbak.com

REUSABLE SNACK BAGS AND SANDWICH WRAPPERS

Lunchskins: Cute-as-a-button designs on reusable snack and sandwich bags. www.lunchskins.com

Itzy Ritzy: Reusable bags with stylish graphic prints that close with a zipper. www.itzyritzy.com

Resources

I relied on a number of sources for research and inspiration in writing this book, many of which might prove useful to you as well, especially since what we know about food and nutrition changes on an ongoing basis.

NUTRIENT DATA AND DIETARY GUIDELINES

USDA National Nutrient Database for Standard Reference, ndb.nal.usda.gov

USDA Food and Nutrition Information Center, fnic.nal.usda.gov

USDA Choose My Plate guidelines and tools, www.choosemyplate.gov

Understanding Nutrition, Eleanor Noss Whitney and Sharon Rady Rolfes (West Publishing, 2007)

FOOD AND NUTRITION INSIGHT

Centers for Disease Control and Prevention, www.cdc.gov/nutrition

Center for Science in the Public Interest, www.cspinet.org

National Institutes of Health Medline Plus, www.nlm.nih.gov/medlineplus

Dr. Andrew Weil, www.drweil.com

What to Eat: An Aisle-by-Aisle Guide to Savvy Food Choices and Good Eating, Marion Nestle (North Point Press, 2006)

The Wellness Encyclopedia of Food and Nutrition, Sheldon Margen, M.D., and the Editors of the University of California at Berkeley Wellness letter (Rebus, 1992)

FOOD SAFETY

USDA Food Safety and Inspection Service, www.fsis.usda.gov/Home/index.asp

FDA Food Safety, www.fda.gov/Food/Food Safety/default.htm

USDA Food Safety Hotline, 1-888-674-6854 or www.AskKaren.gov

SUSTAINABILITY

Sustainable Table, www.sustainabletable.org

Monterey Bay Aquarium Seafood Watch, www.montereybayaquarium.org/cr/seafood watch.aspx

CHEMICALS, PESTICIDES, ENVIRONMENTAL POLLUTANTS

Environmental Working Group, www.ewg.org

Natural Resources Defense Council, www.nrdc.org

Acknowledgments

First and foremost, I'd like to thank the many lovely ladies (and a few gents) who have become part of the Mom's Kitchen Handbook community. I so appreciate you tuning in, sharing recipes, swapping stories, and participating in this effort to nourish our families with good food and heaps of love.

To my girlfriends who support and inspire me every day, including Suzanne Bergeron, you always keep me grounded and help me remember that not every home cook has a Japanese mandolin or collection of exotic salts. Alison Eastwood, my fellow dietitian and longtime friend, you read and edited *every* page despite three little ones underfoot. Alyssa Ure, the design talent behind my blog, you always keep me on my toes in the pretty department. Leigh Oshirak, you have gone way beyond the call of duty to help out a friend. I will absorb every ounce of professional brilliance you are willing to throw my way.

To my three stalwart recipe testers and their children: Claire Bobrow, Jane MacKay, and Pam Rupright, you always received my recipes with enthusiasm and gave me honest feedback and delicious ideas. I'm also grateful to the handful of other recipe testers who pitched in.

To Kate Haisch, my nutrition intern. I so appreciate your research and feedback, and I love that you managed to do it all with a baby on your hip.

To Sara Catalan, who kept me company in the kitchen, tested my recipes, and kept an eye on my brood as I worked to pull this project together.

To Carole Bidnick, my agent. I'm so very grateful for you, who took on my tiny project and never made me feel less important than any of your big-name clients. I always feel like you are in my corner.

To the team that brought this book to life: Bill LeBlond at Chronicle Books, you seemed to know I had something to offer long before I knew it myself. Amy Treadwell, my editor, you gently walked me through this first book with such patience. Jennifer Martiné, fab photographer, you were so warm, welcoming, and fun to work with. To all the other folks at Chronicle: Alice Chau in design, Doug Ogan and Claire Fletcher in managing editorial, Jane Tunks in copy editing, Tera Killip in production, and the publicity duo of Peter Perez and David Hawk.

To Marion Nestle, I will never forget being summoned by the dean of the NYU nutrition department and told I had talent as a writer. It was just the boost of confidence (and connections) I needed to send me on my way as a food writer, a career I love.

Much gratitude to Sarah Copeland, mom, cookbook author, and friend, you inspired my whole Mom's Kitchen Handbook journey just by being your lovely and talented self.

To all the wonderful cooks in my family who've taught me what I know, most especially my fabulous parents, my megatalented siblings, and all my beloved aunties. A special thanks to my sister-in-law Alison Sullivan, pastry chef extraordinaire, whose fingerprints are all over my desserts.

And of course, to my hubby, Joe (a.k.a. "Mr. Mom's Kitchen"): my number-one fan, enthusiastic diner, and always willing unpaid editor. Thank goodness one of us knows their way around a grammar rulebook. I love you.

Saving the best for last, I'm most especially grateful to my three spectacular daughters—Isabelle, Rosie, and Virginia—without whom I would never know how to write a lunch-box book. You are the best critics, taste testers, and cheerleaders I could hope for. I'm one lucky mom.

Index

Table of Equivalents

LIQUID MEASUREMENTS

U.S.	METRIC
1/4 teaspoon	1.25 milliliters
1/2 teaspoon	2.5 milliliters
1 teaspoon	5 milliliters
1 tablespoon (3 teaspoons)	15 milliliters
1 fluid ounce (2 tablespoons)	30 milliliters
1/4 cup	60 milliliters
1/3 cup	80 milliliters
1/2 cup	120 milliliters
1 cup	240 milliliters
1 pint (2 cups)	480 milliliters
1 quart (4 cups, 32 ounces)	960 milliliters
1 gallon (4 quarts)	3.84 liters

DRY MEASUREMENTS

U.S.	METRIC
1 ounce (by weight)	28 grams
1 pound	448 grams
2.2 pounds	1 kilogram

LENGTHS

U.S.	METRIC
1/8 inch	3 millimeters
1/4 inch	6 millimeters
1/2 inch	12 millimeters
1 inch	2.5 centimeters

OVEN TEMPERATURE

FAHRENHEIT	CELSIUS	GAS
250	120	1/2
275	140	1
300	150	2
325	160	3
350	180	4
375	190	5
400	200	6
425	220	7
450	230	8
475	240	9
500	260	10

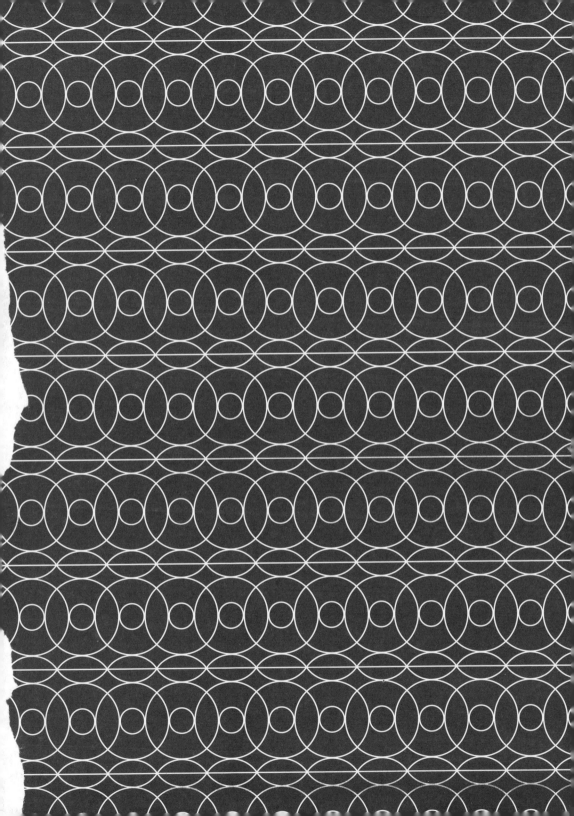